Northwest Coast Indian Art

AN ANALYSIS OF FORM

Native Art of the Pacific Northwest

A Bill Holm Center Series

The mission of this publication series is to foster appreciation and understanding of Pacific Northwest Native art and culture.

In the Spirit of the Ancestors: Contemporary Northwest Coast Art at the Burke Museum, edited by Robin K. Wright and Kathryn Bunn-Marcuse

Return to the Land of the Head Hunters: Edward S. Curtis, the Kwakwa̲ka̲'wakw, and the Making of Modern Cinema, edited by Brad Evans and Aaron Glass

Northwest Coast Indian Art: An Analysis of Form, 50th Anniversary Edition, by Bill Holm

Northwest Coast Indian Art

AN ANALYSIS OF FORM

50TH ANNIVERSARY EDITION

Bill Holm

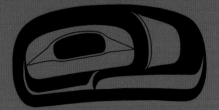

BILL HOLM CENTER FOR THE
STUDY OF NORTHWEST COAST ART
Burke Museum, Seattle

in association with

UNIVERSITY OF WASHINGTON PRESS
Seattle and London

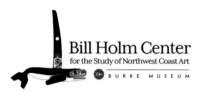

© 1965 by the University of Washington Press
50th Anniversary Edition © 2015 by the University of Washington Press
Printed and bound in South Korea
Design by Thomas Eykemans
Composed in Chaparral, typeface designed by Carol Twombly
18   5 4 3 2

BILL HOLM CENTER FOR THE STUDY OF NORTHWEST COAST ART
Burke Museum of Natural History and Culture
www.burkemuseum.org/bhc

UNIVERSITY OF WASHINGTON PRESS
www.washington.edu/uwpress

Library of Congress Cataloging-in-Publication Data record available at
https://lccn.loc.gov/2014019719

ISBN 978-0-295-99427-7

Contents

Illustrations

Collections
Consulted

Alaska State Museum, Juneau, Alaska*

American Museum of Natural History, New York

British Museum, London*

Burke Museum, Seattle, Washington (Washington State Museum)*

Canadian Museum of History, Ottawa, Ontario
(formerly National Museum of Canada)*

Denver Art Museum, Denver, Colorado*

The Field Museum of Natural History, Chicago, Illinois
(formerly Chicago Natural History Museum)*

Museum of Northern British Columbia, Prince Rupert,
British Columbia*

Museum of Vancouver, Vancouver, British Columbia
(formerly Vancouver City Museum)

National Museum of the American Indian, Washington, D.C.
(formerly Museum of the American Indian, Heye Foundation)

Portland Art Museum, Portland, Oregon*

Royal British Columbia Museum, Victoria, British Columbia
(formerly Provincial Museum)*

Seattle Art Museum, Seattle, Washington*

Skagway Museum, Skagway, Alaska

Statens Etnografiska Museum, Stockholm, Sweden*

University of British Columbia Museum of Anthropology,
Vancouver, British Columbia*

Whatcom Museum of History and Art, Bellingham, Washington
(formerly Bellingham Public Museum)

Foreword

Robin K. Wright
Kathryn Bunn-Marcuse

BILL HOLM CENTER
FOR THE STUDY OF
NORTHWEST COAST ART
Burke Museum

THIS BOOK WAS FIRST PUBLISHED FIFTY YEARS AGO AS MONO-graph no. 1 in a series of Burke Museum and University of Washington Press publications. The first four books of this nine-book series were by Bill Holm: monograph no. 2, *Edward S. Curtis in the Land of the War Canoes: A Pioneer Cinematographer in the Pacific Northwest* (Holm and Quimby 1980); monograph no. 3, *Smoky-Top: The Art and Times of Willie Seaweed* (Holm 1983); monograph no. 4, *Spirit and Ancestor: A Century of Northwest Coast Indian Art at the Burke Museum* (Holm 1987).

Since its publication in 1965, *Northwest Coast Indian Art: An Analysis of Form* has become one of the all-time best-selling books published by the University of Washington Press. The Bill Holm Center at the Burke Museum is pleased that this 50th anniversary edition is among the first publications in the center's new series, Native Art of the Pacific Northwest. This new series includes *In the Spirit of the Ancestors: Contemporary Northwest Coast Art at the Burke Museum* (Wright and Bunn-Marcuse 2013) and *Return to the Land of the Head Hunters: Edward S. Curtis, the Kwakwaka'wakw, and the Making of Modern Cinema* (Evans and Glass 2014), sequels to the Burke monographs no. 4 and no. 2, respectively.

During the past fifty years, the history of Northwest Coast art has been a rich and full one, led by an amazing array of talented artists who have studied the art of their ancestors and brought it forward into the twenty-first century with innovation and cultural significance. As a preface to this edition, we have invited a few of those artists to offer their own thoughts on the importance of this book and on Bill Holm. Each of these artists chose to reflect on his or her early interactions with Holm and the easy dialogues they shared about Northwest Coast art and form.

The design system described in this book is central to painted, carved, and woven art forms from the northern Northwest Coast. An understanding of the design elements is critical to weavers of *naaxiin* textiles. Evelyn Vanderhoop, a skilled Haida weaver, reflects on making her first full robe and on Holm's role in its creation. In the years since that first robe, Evelyn has returned to Seattle as a demonstrator at the Burke Museum and as a Bill Holm Center research fellow, studying the old textiles in the Burke's collection and sharing her knowledge with students and the public at the University of Washington.

Joe David is a Tla-o-qui-aht artist long dedicated to the vitality of Nuu-chah-nulth art and ceremony. His art reflects a deep commitment to his spirituality and cultural heritage. Like many others, David met Bill Holm through the latter's work at the Burke Museum and his classes on Northwest Coast art at the University of Washington. Holm welcomed artists and visitors to sit in on his lectures. David's recollections note the visual utility of *An Analysis of Form* for artists interested in the northern formline "alphabet."

Nathan Jackson is a master Tlingit artist and a leader of the Lukaax.adí clan. He has taken on many apprentices over the years, using Holm's book as a reference and study guide that brings together examples from the nineteenth-century masters.

Robert Davidson is an internationally renowned artist whose work is grounded in the formline grammar of older Haida art. His work reveals careful reflection on the forms of Northwest Coast painting and an ability to push formal elements into new relationships, ones that are distinctly different from older examples and yet seemingly natural extensions of the same formal principles. Davidson's reflection illustrates the kind of understanding of the art form that comes only from spending a lifetime looking deeply at the art—a dedication that both Holm and Davidson have shared with the public in their own ways.

Since his retirement in 1985, Bill Holm has painted many canvases depicting historical scenes of the Northwest Coast, Plains, and Plateau regions and has continued to do research about the art of these areas, and to teach, speak, and publish about it. His eight books have won scholarly acclaim and recognition, including four Washington State Governor's Writers Awards and two special governor's awards. His achievements as an artist were celebrated in *Sun Dogs and Eagle Down: The Indian Paintings of Bill Holm* (Brown and Averill 2000). In 2001, he was honored with a certificate of appreciation from the Tlingit, Haida, and Tsimshian peoples of Southeast Alaska through the Sealaska Heritage Institute. The Native American Art Studies Association recognized him with its Honor Award in 1991. The University of Washington College of Arts and Sciences honored him with a Distinguished Achievement Award in 1994 and the Timeless Award for distinguished alumni for outstanding service and achievement in 2012. The University of Washington also selected him to give the prestigious annual University Faculty Lecture in 2003. In 2008 he received an honorary doctoral degree from the University of Alaska, Fairbanks.

We are pleased to present this 50th anniversary volume of *Northwest Coast Indian Art: An Analysis of Form* with the original text, enhanced color diagrams and images, updated captions with current museum information, and a new preface by Bill Holm. Thank you to Sara Jo Kinslow, who carefully colorized all the diagrams, and to Ashley Verplank McClelland for tracking down and getting permissions for the color photographs. We hope it will continue to be as useful in the future as it has been for the past fifty years.

Artists' Reflections

Evelyn Vanderhoop

THE DESIGNS OF THE *NAAXIIN* ARE BOUNDED BY BOTH THE pentagonal format and the horizontal and vertical warps and wefts used to create a chief's robe. The unique angled ovoids and U-shaped forms are a dialectal variant of the visual language of the Northwest Coast, which has been studied and defined by Bill Holm in his groundbreaking book *Northwest Coast Indian Art: An Analysis of Form.* Reading this influential book, I was better able to comprehend the designs that stretched and filled the textile matrix of the *naaxiin*.

In the early 1970s, when I was still in university, I was bold enough, during a visit to the University of Washington, to go to Bill Holm's office and introduce myself as the granddaughter of Selina Peratrovich, a Haida weaver known to Bill. Offered that preface, he was kind enough to give me his time. I had studied his book and used it for a book-review assignment in my art history course at Western Washington University, in Bellingham, and I was elated to meet the author of the book that I knew was in the libraries of all Northwest Coast carvers and artists. It wasn't until the late 1990s, as I transformed from a painter to a weaver, that the concepts discussed in that influential book, as well as its respected author, would affect my own art.

When I received my first commission for a full-size robe, it was for a replication of a robe exhibited in the American Museum of Natural History in New York City. An image of the robe appeared in the book *From the Land of the Totem Poles: The Northwest Coast Indian Art Collection at the American Museum of Natural History,* by Aldona Jonaitis, but I traveled to New York City in order to examine the robe itself, which I was able to do for only one day. The robe was behind glass, and I studied it for hours. I measured it; I counted the warps that showed through the worn sea otter fur; I estimated the warp size. It was exquisite, with its fine mountain-goat-wool wefts and its soft, aged hues. I was overwhelmed—near, yet unable to touch or photograph it or turn it around to see its technique-revealing back.

I knew that taking detailed notes was essential, so I reached into my purse for paper on which to write. I often joked about my purse being a "black hole": material entered it, never to be found again. But there at the museum, I pulled out a sheet of paper folded in quarters that, when unfolded, revealed a photocopy of the robe before me. It was serendipitous. I had no idea how or when that image was placed in my purse. To me, it was a sign from the universe that I was doing what I was supposed to be doing. Any doubt I may have had was gone. The robe I was about to begin making was meant to be, and it would be my guide.

After that day of study in New York, I returned home with my notes and a few poor photographs showing fuzzy details through reflected glare. Two hundred years ago a *naaxiin* robe weaver would have been given a painted cedar pattern board along with the request to weave this important and powerful chief's garment. I expressed my dilemma to the collectors who had commissioned the *naaxiin* robe replication, and shortly afterward I received a large paper pattern from them. It was huge, not in proportion to the original robe in New York. I called to thank them, but also to say I could not use it. As a novice robe creator, I did not feel I could deviate from the proportions of the original as I created the replication. My sister, Holly Churchill, was visiting me at my home near Seattle when I told her about my need for an at-scale pattern design for the robe. She immediately thought of Bill Holm, with whom she had become friends while he was in Ketchikan teaching a carving class at the Totem Heritage Center, where she also teaches. He had carved a wooden hat form in exchange for her teaching him a weaving technique.

We went to his home, and she told him about my problem. He turned to his vast home library and found a book with the robe's image. Appraising the problem, he asked us if we could leave him for a while and return in a few hours, and so we did. Within that short amount of time, he had scanned the book image, calculated the proportions, and printed multiple eight-and-a-half-by-eleven-inch sheets, which he had taped together to form an at-scale paper "pattern board." I was thrilled, and so thankful for such an esteemed man's assistance. It was another sign that I was on the right path. I used that paper pattern board for two and a half years, and it became well worn. It traveled with me to the various places where I demonstrated weaving. I loved to point out my pattern board and tell people how Bill Holm had helped me.

When the robe was finished, it was brought out at a feast at the Daybreak Star Indian Cultural Center in Seattle. It is customary to acknowledge everyone who takes part in creating a robe, and of course Bill Holm's contribution was acknowledged. He was out of the country at that time, however, and unable to attend. Later, I brought the completed robe to his home so he could see what I had done while following his paper pattern board. He complimented me, but he added that he initially had had doubts that my replication of the complex chief's robe would be completed. He had not been aware that I felt the robe was a willing guide, and that his creating my pattern board had also been a sign that my weaving the robe and completing it was sanctioned by mystical providence.

Many years later, during a slide presentation of my *naaxiin* weaving at the Burke Museum, I was able to again acknowledge Bill as an early inspiration for completing that first robe. Bill and his wife, Marty, were in attendance, and I was glad of the opportunity to not only thank him again for inspiring me but also thank him for his influence on weavers as a result of his research into the Northwest Coast art and textiles. Dorica Jackson and Cheryl Samuel had shared with me their accounts of how Bill Holm had, through his professorship at the University of Washington, helped them and other weavers advance their knowledge of the history and techniques of the *naaxiin*. Cheryl went on to further research the early mountain-goat-wool weaving of the northern Northwest Coast, and this research culminated in the current revival of ancient techniques used in Ravenstail weaving.

Cheryl also went on to teach my mother, Delores Churchill, *naaxiin* and Ravenstail weaving. Both of these women were my mentors, and they taught me the Northwest Coast textiles. My sister, Holly, also benefited by Bill's willingness to share his research. From his work, she learned about cedar bark clothing, and now she shares that knowledge with students in her classes and workshops. A 1982 article published in the *American Indian Art Magazine,* "A Wooling Mantle Neatly Wrought: The Early Historic Record of Northwest Coast Pattern-Twined Textiles—1774–1850," by Bill Holm, broadened my interest in the precontact cultural use of mountain-goat-wool textiles, and I began my quest into that history. Because of Bill Holm's published works and personal friendships, the traditional formline art, weaving, and history are better understood by collectors, artists, weavers, and students of the cultures of the Pacific Northwest Coast. *Haw'aa*, Bill.

· · ·

Joe David

I CAME ACROSS BILL HOLM'S BOOK *NORTHWEST COAST INDIAN Art: An Analysis of Form* in Seattle, in the summer of 1970. I've heard it said that when a student is ready, a teacher will find him. And I was ready! In fact, I came across the book and Duane Pasco the same day, in the very same hour. Pasco was carving a totem pole at the Seattle Center's food pavilion. I showed him Holm's book, and his response was, "It's a good book!" And it has been *the good book on the art*, often, in fact, called *the bible* of Northwest Coast art.

I tried reading it but quickly found that words were not to be my method of understanding the subject matter. But I liked the pictures, the illustrations. Those I could read! I saw the alphabet (Robert Davidson's term) clearly defined. And I could see that the bar was set and my goal was clear.

I went about it freehand. I did not attempt to train my brain and hand to trace Holm's illustrations and photo examples. At first my designs were clumsy and stiff—it would be years before my Northwest Coast calligraphy showed some ease and grace. But it helped greatly that I sat in on Bill Holm's classes on Northwest Coast art and culture at the University of Washington. Bill soon became a constant in my universe, and I was in no hurry. Osmosis, I believe, is a big factor in cultural dynamics and is largely ignored by those who believe that brains 'r' us, and that the rest of the body is simply mechanics. Consider that there is now a generation who understand the art forms fairly well without ever having seen "the writing" or met Holm. In other words, they are simply involved in doing the art. In fact, Bill Holm never intended his study to be a how-to book, and he has probably stated that fact more than anything else about it. Having long since mastered the northern alphabet, I, like a lot of other artists, still look back to the book these many years later, but as a place to visit rather than as a reference.

I mentioned that, many years ago, I refused to continue reading the book (and I've never actually read the entire thing). But before I put it down, I tore the cover off and framed it. And to this day I always have it hanging in my studio space. It was my very first Bill Holm print, and it remains a presence in my creative realm.

My favorite story about Holm's book happened when my wild, crazy friend Goof (Godfrey Stephens) approached Bill at our family potlatch at Tofino in the fall of 1977. Goof told him he had owned a copy of his book until the tide came and washed it out to sea. And Bill replied, "That's the best thing anyone has ever said about my book!"

. . .

Nathan Jackson

IN REFLECTING BACK ON THE 1960S, WHEN BILL FIRST CAME to Haines, Alaska, I recall that he demonstrated his work and talked about other works of museum quality. His textbook at that time was his new book, *Northwest Coast Indian Art: An Analysis of Form*. In 1962, I had gone to the Institute of American Indian Arts, in Santa Fe, New Mexico, where I found a lot of books illustrating the art form. But the principles of this art weren't clear to me until after I heard Bill's lecture in Haines.

Around that time, 1965, Carl Heinmiller of Alaska Indian Arts, in Haines, challenged me to do some designing. Bill's book made it a lot easier for me to create new designs. My wife has reminded me that I told her about being back east, looking at Northwest Coast stuff in museums and trying to figure out how everything went together. When I found Bill's book, I was amazed, because it was all laid out right there! I still have a hardback copy of the book, signed by Bill, in which he drew a raven-head design.

Most of the people who want to apprentice with me find that drawing is a challenge, and so I have used the book to point out the rules established by some of the older Northwest Coast artists, whether we're discussing bentwood box designs or a panel design or any other design. In teaching my apprentices, I use the template technique I learned from Bill.

Back in the 1960s, I once asked Bill how to properly use an adze, because I could tell it wasn't being done correctly there in Haines. He showed me how. In Haines, Bill opened my eyes to two-dimensional art. That was also the beginning of a long friendship.

. . .

Robert Davidson

THE SECRET OF GOOD DESIGN IN HAIDA AND NORTHWEST Coast art is to learn how to look at the shapes created by the old masters. Once you learn how the shapes work, you can interpret them to make your own creations. Looking at a good design without knowing what to look for is not going to help you. Good design embodies well-refined shapes, good composition, positive elements in balance with negative spaces, color, movement, a well-balanced skeleton or formline defining the character, and a wow factor. Through his book, Bill Holm helped many artists launch their careers in the vocabulary of Northwest Coast art. Because of this book, many practicing artists today have a jump-start in learning the formula of Northwest Coast art.

I have to tell a little story here: One time when I was working with Bill Reid he was designing a gold box, and he knew a person down in Seattle by the name of Bill Holm. Bill Holm had an encyclopedia of images in his mind. Bill Reid consulted with Bill Holm on box designs, and I had the privilege of watching Bill Holm doodle about ten designs in an hour's time. That time was the very beginning of my learning the subtleties of Northwest Coast art. As I gained more knowledge from studying the pieces, I recognized that some of the designs Bill Holm had drawn were from his experience of studying classic box designs.

It was absolutely amazing to watch Bill Holm draw and create within that given space. He had unraveled the secrets of Northwest Coast art, which he presents in this book.

Preface to the 50th Anniversary Edition

Bill Holm

AS I LOOK BACK ON FIVE DECADES OF *NORTHWEST COAST Indian Art: An Analysis of Form,* there really isn't much that I would change today. I suppose if I had guessed that it would become a kind of handbook for Northwest Coast Native artists, rather than a somewhat technical analysis of the characteristics of northern Northwest Coast art, I might have written it differently. Probably the first thing I would have changed is the title, adding the word *northern* before *Northwest Coast*. Although the geographic limits of the tradition are stated a number of times in the text, many artists and some others using it have often skipped the words in favor of the pictures. The result has been that many people have assumed the art tradition described was pancoastal.

I probably would change a few terms, too, and perhaps correct a few questionable statements. My goal in inventing terminology was always to create highly descriptive words. That I sometimes failed in this, I regret. For example, the term *salmon-trout's-head* was lifted bodily from George Emmons' list of terms given him by Tlingit weavers (Emmons, 1907:Fig. 559). I tend now to call this and related design elements *elaborated inner ovoids*, since they almost never represent a fish's head. Similarly, the design representing a wide, frontal face with long, narrow nostrils, which I referred to as a *double-eye structure*, I now call a *two-step structure*, referring to the unique arrangement of the formlines delineating the corners of the mouth and nostrils. And a related term—the former *single-eye structure*—is now the *one-step structure*. On the other hand, I still hold to the descriptive terms *tertiary line* and *T-shaped relief* over the terms often used by contemporary Northwest Coast artists, *fine line* and *trigon*, since I believe the old terms better describe the figures' functions.

As I became familiar with the characteristic shapes and arrangements of the elements of northern Northwest Coast two-dimensional art, I realized there was a sort of grammar or syntax to it not unlike that of a written language. There were "rules" that transcended tribal and linguistic boundaries on the north-

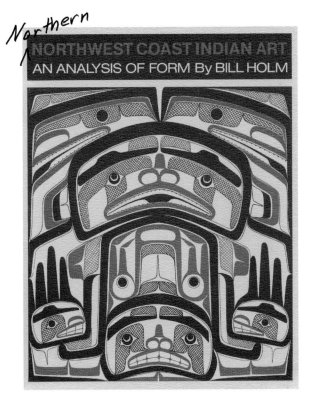

Northern

Bill Holm's "corrected" cover image of the paperback version of *Northwest Coast Indian Art: An Analysis of Form.*

ern coast, and these rules were followed with remarkable uniformity by artists of all the tribes in the area. Like a written language, the visual language allowed artists to produce individual variations while still conforming to the rules. And just as the proper and proficient use of writing doesn't guarantee a great poem or gripping novel, following the "rules" of the northern Northwest Coast formline doesn't automatically result in great art. That is left to the artist.

A short history of the genesis of *Northwest Coast Indian Art: An Analysis of Form* is included in the preface to the original edition. Here I would like to elaborate just a bit. After completing my work for a master of fine arts degree in painting under the GI Bill, I cast about for a job. I liked teaching, so I went back to school to qualify for a teaching certificate. A requirement at that time was that I return to school after a year of teaching. By that time I had a pretty good understanding of the characteristics of the formline system, so I approached my longtime friend Dr. Erna Gunther, then chair of the anthropology department and director of the Washington State Museum (now the Burke Museum of Natural History and Culture), with the proposal that I take a graduate research course from her and write a paper on the subject of "the structure of Northwest Coast Indian two-dimensional art." Dr. Gunther readily agreed, and the result was the basis for this book. The paper lay fallow for half a dozen years, until I was urged by friends to publish it. This sounded like a good idea, but I began to realize that it was incomplete; it lacked any kind of documentation, all of which I carried in my head. I went to Dr. Gunther for advice. This was in the days before personal computers, and she suggested that I try Keysort cards, a manual information-storage system, to record characteristics and organize the results. I recorded the characteristics of 392 specimens on 400 cards and used the results to fine-tune my conclusions. Then, what to do next?

Things Happen

I had no idea of how to proceed toward publishing the study. One day I was in a laboratory in the Burke Museum, visiting a friend who had generously let me use a picture of a contemporary silver bracelet he owned as an illustration of how the design system had broken down (Fig. 66B). Dr. Walter Fairservis, who was then the director of the Burke, was in the room with us and heard our conversation. He came over and asked me what we were talking about. A specialist in

Asian and Middle Eastern art, Dr. Fairservis was at that time being unfairly criticized by some members of the public for not exhibiting more of the museum's Northwest Coast collections. I briefly described my study to him. He turned, picked up the phone, dialed it, and said, "Hello, Don [Don Ellegood, director of the University of Washington Press], we have a great manuscript here on the art of the Indians of the Northwest Coast."

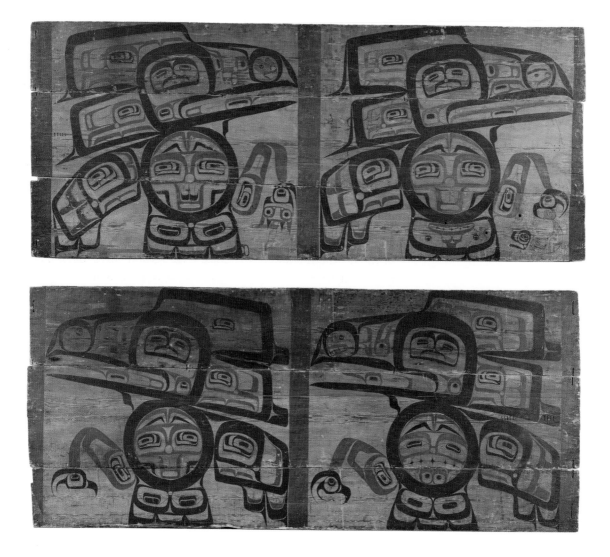

1 The Raven Screens of the Huna, Tlingit. The dramatic story of their acquisition by the Denver Art Museum, which literally rescued them from a fencemaker's saw, is briefly told in Feder and Malin, 1962. Painted on cedar boards in black and red, they are among the highest achievements of the Indian artists of the northern coast. Unknown Tlingit artist, House Screen, about 1850, Denver Art Museum Collection: Purchase from Henry Moses, 1939.140.1-1939.140.2. Photograph © Denver Art Museum.

Preface to the Original Edition

THE RAVEN SCREENS OF THE HUNA ARE AMONG THE MASTER-pieces of Northwest Coast Indian art. When I first stood before these powerful murals the virtuosity of the artist overwhelmed me. I marveled at his mastery of the space provided by two fourteen-foot panels of cedar, at the continuity and power of the broad, black form-lines delineating the representations of Raven, and at the subtle variations in form and detail of each of the four figures (Fig. 1).

In a richly refined silver bracelet (Fig. 65) or slate chest (Fig. 2) by Charles Edensaw, the sensitivity and skill of a master Haida crafts-man are apparent. The endless detail and superb craftsmanship of the "Rain Wall" of the Whale House at Klukwan are amazing (Fig. 67). A long parade of masterworks from the hands of Indian artists of the northern tribes of the Coast—chests and boxes, dishes, rat-tles, crest hats, and more—excite admiration. Although varied in provenience, material, size, and purpose, these pieces are related to a surprising degree in the organization and form of their two-di-mensional surface decoration. It is my goal here to define some of the principles that relate these pieces to each other.

The preliminary work for this study began over twenty years ago when an intense interest in Northwest Coast Indian dances led me into the making of masks and ceremonial paraphernalia. From the beginning the effort was not to reproduce specific pieces but to synthesize the characteristics of many related specimens in order to arrive at a result which was "original" and yet within the conven-tions of style, subject, material, and technique of a particular tribe. Gradually I developed a realization of the system of principles that governed certain aspects of Northwest Coast Indian art.

When I attempted to reconstruct the rules upon which this system of principles was based, however, it became apparent that, although my conclusions seemed logical on the basis of the material examined, there was no real documentation to substantiate them. Consequently a new start was made: many of the pieces upon which my original study was based were re-examined, and many more not previously seen were included. Characteristics of each item exam-ined were recorded on a check list and the data subsequently trans-ferred to Keysort cards. Four hundred examples of Northwest Coast art were coded. Analysis of this material has indicated some addi-tions to and modifications of the original conclusions.

In this effort I am indebted to many helpful institutions and individuals, particularly Dr. Erna Gunther, former Director of the

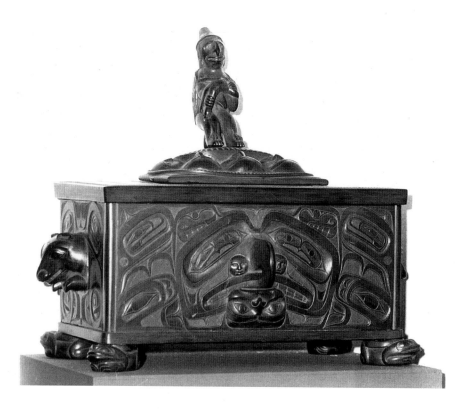

2 Argillite chest, Haida. Charles Edensaw carved and constructed this elaborate chest from slabs of argillite, a carbonaceous shale. Edensaw excelled in this craft, which dates from the early years of the nineteenth century. Argillite carvings were almost always intended for sale to white men. Image cpn10622 courtesy of Royal B.C. Museum, B.C. Archives.

Washington State Museum, for her encouragement, assistance, and helpful criticism, and the use of the Washington State Museum's collection and facilities. Much credit is due the help and cooperation of Wilson Duff, Curator of Anthropology, the British Columbia Provincial Museum, where more than one third of the specimens studied are to be found. Also included in this study are pieces from the collections of the National Museum of Canada; the University of British Columbia Museum of Anthropology; the Alaska State Museum; the Museum of Northern British Columbia; the American Museum of Natural History; the City Museum of Vancouver; the Denver Art Museum; the Chicago Natural History Museum; the Museum of the American Indian, Heye Foundation; the Lipsett Museum of Vancouver, B.C.; and the Portland Art Museum, as well as articles from the collections of many private individuals to whom I express my appreciation.

Ideally, a study of this sort should lean heavily on information from Indian artists trained in the tradition that fostered the art. Unfortunately, I was unable to locate a qualified informant from the area covered, i.e., the coastal region from Bella Coola to Yakutat Bay. That there may be some still living is not questioned, but con-

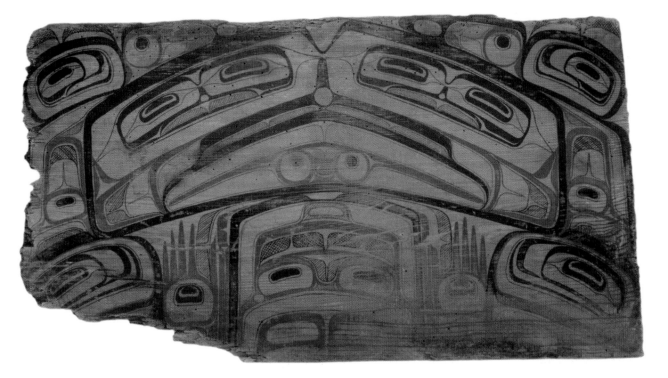

3 Fragment of a painted coffin, Bella Bella. Canadian Museum of History, catalogue number VII EE 29, image number S94-33644.

temporary work seen from the area reveals a lack of understanding by Indian craftsmen of the principles that are the subject of this study. Bill Reid, perhaps the best Haida craftsman working today, thoroughly understands the art, but he, like the author, has reconstructed the rules from examination and analysis of old pieces. Nevertheless, I am deeply indebted to him for his suggestions and insight.

A number of living Kwakiutl trained as artists before the collapse of the apprentice system are known to me. In spite of this, and in spite of the richness of Kwakiutl collections in the museums visited, no specimen known to be Kwakiutl (that is, Southern Kwakiutl as distinguished from Bella Bella, Haisla, and Xaihais of the north [Fig. 3]) has been included in the formulation of these conclusions, and only a few have been coded for purposes of comparison. Kwakiutl art, although closely related to the art of the northern tribes, varies from it so much that a typical Kwakiutl piece could not be recorded on the check list used in this analysis. A few notes from Kwakiutl informants and references have been included where they shed light on techniques, attitudes, and materials common to the whole coast.

Northwest Coast Indian Art

AN ANALYSIS OF FORM

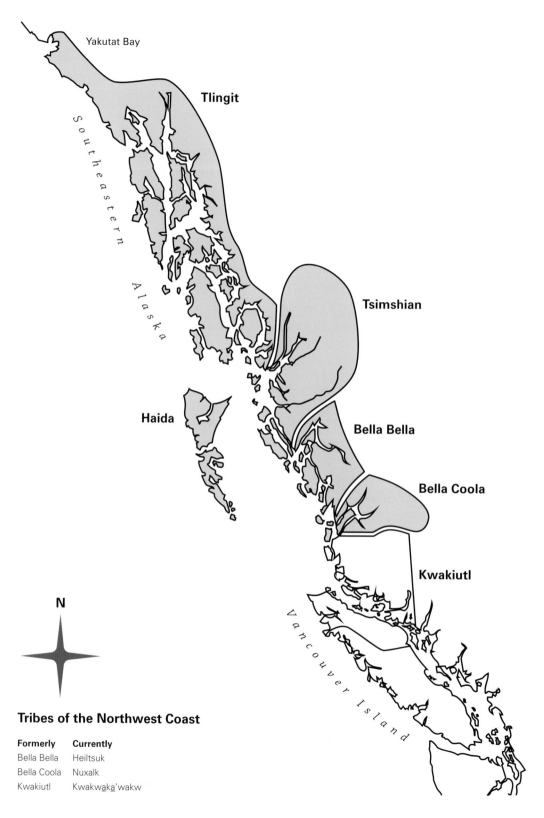

Yakutat Bay

Tlingit

Southeastern

Alaska

Tsimshian

Haida

Bella Bella

Bella Coola

Kwakiutl

Vancouver Island

N

Tribes of the Northwest Coast

Formerly	Currently
Bella Bella	Heiltsuk
Bella Coola	Nuxalk
Kwakiutl	Kwakw<u>aka</u>'wakw

Historical
Background

THE PREHISTORY OF NORTHWEST COAST INDIAN ART IS VERY obscure and has fostered a great deal of conjecture. To some students the art has seemed very recent, dependent on introduced tool iron for its full development. Others (Adam, 1936; Barbeau, 1953; Covarrubias, 1954; Fraser, 1962) have seen a relationship to Asian or early Chinese art. The thesis that the art as we know it may have had a long history of local origin and development has been propounded by Gunther (1962:40) and Duff (1956:104–10; 1964:84–94). Recent developments in archeology and the science of dating may throw a good deal of light on the subject. Although it is not within the scope of this study to enter the field of historical speculation, a brief investigation of the state of development of northern Northwest Coast two-dimensional art at the beginning of the historical period is pertinent.

In 1787 Captain George Dixon reached the Queen Charlotte Islands. He was one of the first white men actually to contact the Haida, and he collected from them, among other specimens, a beautifully carved wooden bowl, now in the collection of the British Museum (Fig. 4; Dixon, 1789:Figs. 1 and 2 opposite p. 188; Inverarity, 1950:Fig. 197). This bowl, in the form of a human figure, is elaborated with shallow relief carving that exactly conforms to the organization and conventions of the best Haida work of a century later.

Another fine piece from the early contact period that attests to the high state of development of the art at that time is a headdress plaque collected by Captain Malaspina between 1790 and 1795 and now in the Museo Arqueológico in Madrid (Paalen, 1943:19). In this striking piece the wings of the hominoid thunderbird are designed and carved exactly according to the conventions of classic northern work of the mid-nineteenth century. Of course the carver of the Malaspina headdress and the maker of the Dixon bowl could very likely have had the advantage of metal tools and the influence, for better or worse, of white contact for a considerable period, since the Russians first landed in Alaska in 1741. Nevertheless, the fact that the conventions of the art were so refined and survived the ravages of the following century absolutely intact suggests great stability and, perhaps, antiquity.

Similarly, the uses to which this art was put changed very little during those one hundred years. The changes that took place were of degree rather than substance, like the remarkable florescence

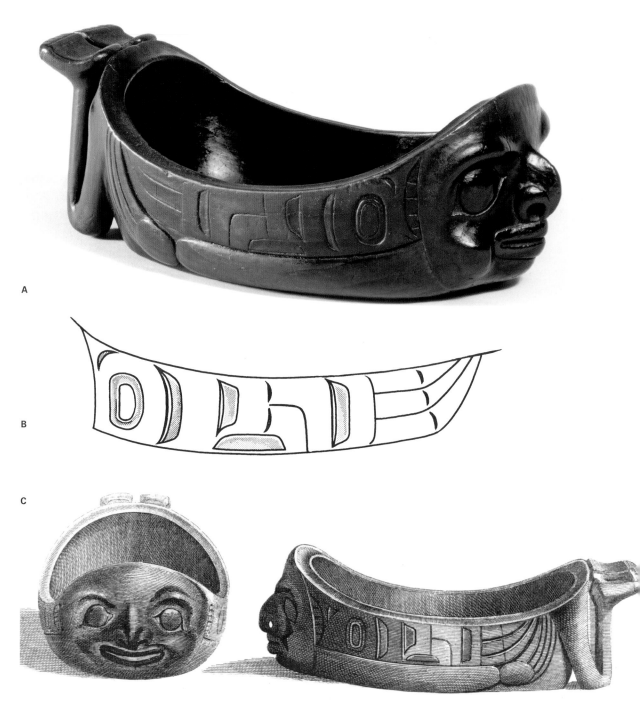

A

B

C

4 (A) Carved wooden bowl, Haida. Collected by Captain Dixon in 1787, this bowl is perhaps the earliest documented example extant of the use of two-dimensional surface decoration described in this study. Image NWC.25 © The Trustees of the British Museum. (B) Two-dimensional detail of Dixon's bowl, drawn from photographs. (C) Engraving of Dixon's bowl (Dixon, 1789). The engraver was unaware of the formline structure of the design, as a comparison of the engraving with the original bowl reveals.

of the totem pole, which certainly existed at the time of contact, although fewer in numbers and less imposing than later, if we interpret the statements of early seamen correctly. A graphic description of the two-dimensional art of the natives of Norfolk Sound, and its application, comes to us from Captain Etienne Marchand, under the date of August, 1791:

> The taste of ornament prevails in all the works of their hands; their canoes, their chests, and different little articles of furniture in use among them, are covered with figures which might be taken for a species of hieroglyphics: fishes and other animals, heads of men, and various whimsical designs, are mingled and confounded in order to compose a subject. It, undoubtedly, will not be expected that these figures should be perfectly regular, and the proportions in them exactly observed; for here, every man is a painter and sculptor; yet they are not deficient in a sort of elegance and perfection [Marchand, 1801:345–46].

Marchand's journal also makes several references to large paintings which, from the descriptions, must be house screens of the type whose existence at this period has been questioned (Keithahn, 1962:19). Although some of the following passages have been quoted recently (Barbeau, 1950:804–5), their bearing on this study makes them worth repeating. On a small island on the west coast of the Queen Charlottes, Captain Chanal investigated an old building containing a number of interesting features, including box drums:

> But what particularly attracted the attention of the French, and well deserved to fix it, were two pictures each of which eight or nine feet long, by five high; was composed only of two planks put together. On one of these pictures, is seen represented, in colours rather lively, red, black, and green, the different parts of the human body, painted separately; and the whole surface covered with them. The latter picture appears to be a copy of the former, or perhaps it is the original: it is difficult to decide to which of the two belongs the priority, so much are the features of both effaced by age [Marchand, 1801:396].

Several very explicit references were made to the apparent age (in 1791) of the painted screens. Their use as ceremonial partitions is attested to by the presence of box drums and by Captain Chanal's conclusions. The use of house screens in pairs, as illustrated by the Huna Raven Screens (Fig. 1), is also fairly typical. A number of other examples are known, including several pairs which are still preserved in the Clan Houses in Klukwan, Alaska.

Another passage from the same work contains significant remarks by Surgeon Roblet:

> The habitations are, in general, painted and decorated in various ways; but what was particularly remarkable in that which the French visited, was a picture somewhat like those which they had seen in the fort of redoubt erected in the small island of the Strait, which occupied the head of the apartment, as is seen suspended in the drawing-rooms in Spain, over the Estrado, the picture of the immaculate conception. Surgeon Roblet has described this production of the fine arts of the NORTH-WEST Coast of AMERICA. "Among a great number of figures very much varied, and which at first appeared to me," says he, "to resemble nothing, I distinguished in the middle a human figure which its extraordinary proportions, still more than its size, render monstrous. Its thighs extended horizontally, after the manner of tailors seated, are slim, long, out of all proportion, and form a carpenter's square with the legs which are equally illmade; the arms extended in the form of a cross, and terminated by fingers, slender and bent. The face is twelve (French) inches, from the extremity of the chin to the top of the forehead, and eighteen inches from one ear to the other; it is surmounted by a sort of cap. Dark red" says he, "apple green, and black are here blended with the natural color of the wood, and distributed in symmetrical spots, with sufficient intelligence to afford at a distance an agreeable object." From the description which Surgeon Roblet gives us of this picture, it might be imagined that it somewhat resembles those shapeless essays of an intelligent child, who undertakes, without principles, to draw objects which present themselves to his sight: I remark, however, that voyagers who have frequented the different parts of the NORTH-WEST Coast of AMERICA, often saw there works of painting and sculpture in which proportions were tolerably well observed, and the execution of which bespoke a taste and perfection which we do not expect to find

in countries where the men seem still to have the appearances of savages. But what must astonish most, and I shall resume this observation in the sequel, is to see paintings every where, every where sculpture, among a nation of hunters [Marchand, 1801:417–19].

Roblet's description is remarkably graphic and, allowing for his demonstrated lack of sympathy with the natives and his ethnocentric orientation in matters of art, can be easily visualized in terms of nineteenth-century northern two-dimensional art.

Symbolism and Realism

THE IMPORTANT ROLE THAT SYMBOLISM PLAYS IN NORTHWEST Coast Indian art is readily apparent to the casual observer. With a little familiarity he will recognize that certain design elements, or "symbols" as they are often popularly known, seem to occur again and again. "Eyes," "joints," "ears," and "feathers," delineated with broad black lines, suggest the existence of a "Northwest Coast" style. Increasingly careful scrutiny reveals that, during the period that produced most of the familiar examples of this art, several more or less distinct styles flourished. It soon becomes apparent that the artists in the area stretching roughly from Bella Coola to Yakutat Bay had a highly developed system of art principles that guided their creative activity and went far beyond the system of conventional animal representation described in the literature, most notably in the works of Franz Boas (1897:123–76; 1927:183–298).

Boas and others recognized that there were other principles important to the character of the art, but only those directly concerned with representation have been adequately covered. These were summed up by Adam (1936:8–9) to include (1) stylizing, as opposed to realistic representation; (2) schematic characterization by accentuating certain features; (3) splitting; (4) dislocating split details; (5) representing one creature by two profiles; (6) symmetry (with exceptions); (7) reducing; and (8) the illogical transformation of details into new representations. All these elements are important and basic to Northwest Coast Indian art, but they are, with the exception of number 6, principles of representation rather than of composition, design organization, or form.

Haeberlin (1918:258–64) indicated a direction for research and analysis in the composition of this art. In reference to the well-known principles of "unfolding" (Adam's "splitting") and the "whole" animal, he wrote, "These important principles refer still to the contents of the representations of this art, not really to the relations of forms, for which it would seem to me the term 'artistic' is properly reserved" (Haeberlin, 1918:258–64). Boas (1927:13) pointed out the importance of recognizing this aspect of art in general. He said, "It is essential to bear in mind the twofold source of artistic effect, the one based on form alone, the other on idea associated with form. Otherwise the theory of art will be one-sided."

Symbolic Ambiguity

That even the most abstracted box or Chilkat blanket design is representative in a symbolic sense has long been known, and the principles of representation have been investigated and published (Boas, 1927:183–280; Inverarity, 1950:40–48; and others). The more highly abstracted the design becomes, that is, the more nearly the represented creature, by distortion and rearrangement of parts, fills the given space, the more difficult it becomes to interpret the symbolism accurately. This difficulty is graphically illustrated by the many contradictions in the explanations by Indian informants of the meaning of Chilkat blanket designs, particularly in the lateral panels (Boas in Emmons, 1907:387). Figure 5A illustrates a blanket that is nearly identical to that shown in Emmons' figure 564A, of which the lateral fields are said to "represent a young raven sitting, at the same time the sides and back of the whale."

It is also very difficult to explain satisfactorily the meaning of designs that are fragmentary in character. The designs painted on Haida gambling sticks are of this type. A set of seventy of these sticks is illustrated by Swanton (1909:149–54) and again by Boas (1927:210–16). The effect that seemingly insignificant detail can have on interpretation is illustrated by an explanation by Charles Edensaw, an outstanding Haida artist, of No. 34 of these gambling stick designs. The intent seems quite obviously to be the head and foot of an eagle, but "Edensaw was rather inclined to consider the design on the left as intended to represent the raven's wing, because it has no tongue, and because it is not the proper form of head belonging with the foot on the right!" (Swanton, 1909:152). From these examples it can be seen that the formal element of the designs very often takes on such importance as to overshadow the symbolic element to a point where the symbolism becomes very obscure.

To meet the requirements of space filling demanded by traditional design principles, the artist must introduce decorative elements so "that it is not possible to assign to each and every element that is derived from animal motives a significant function, but . . . many of them are employed regardless of meaning, and used for purely ornamental purposes" (Boas, 1927:279).

Degree of Realism

Northwest Coast art can be divided into a number of general categories, according to the degree of realism in the design. Practically

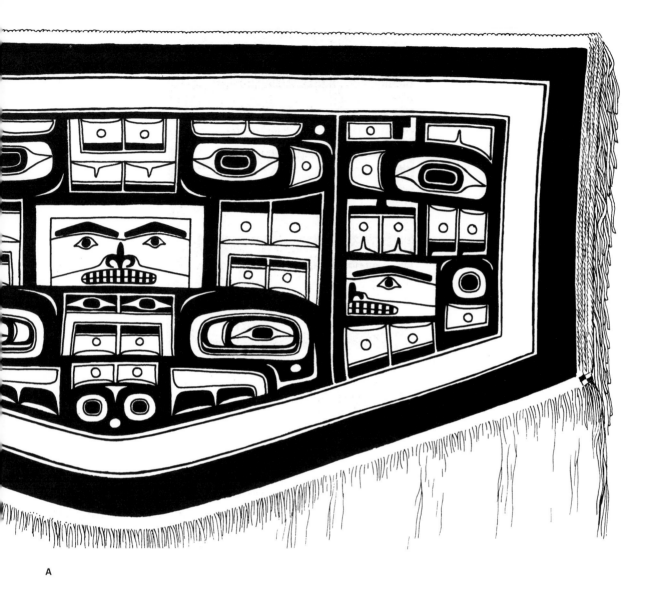

A

5 (A) Woven blanket, Chilkat. Private collection. (B) Hypothetical "copy" of the lateral panel of the blanket in "painting" style. The formline structure of the design in the woven blanket is somewhat obscured by the angularity typical of Chilkat woven designs.

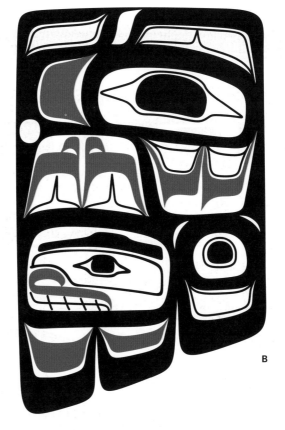

B

no examples of Northwest two-dimensional art are realistic in the ordinary sense. Paintings on shamans' paraphernalia frequently approach representational realism, but even these figures are in the Northwest Coast idiom. The different degrees of realism in this art seem to result not from a variety of concepts of representation but from the artist's preference (more or less strictly bound by tradition) in handling the given space. In each case individual parts of the creature represented assume their conventional form, and the degree of realism (that is, resemblance to the visual form of the creature in nature) achieved is due to the arrangement of these conventionalized body-part symbols.

Three rather loose categories of design can thus be defined for which I use the terms *configurative*, *expansive*, and *distributive*—terms that I believe to be descriptive of the actual handling of the design elements.

1. When the animal to be represented is shown with an essentially animal-like silhouette, perhaps occupying a great part of the decorated field but not distorted so as to fill it entirely, and still exhibits the characteristics of the art style, it can be considered an example of *configurative design* (Fig. 6).

2. When an animal is distorted, split, or rearranged to fit into a given space, but the identity of the essential body parts is apparent and to some extent their anatomical relationship to one another is maintained, the resulting arrangement can be considered an example of *expansive design* (Fig. 7).

3. When the parts of the represented animal are so arranged as completely to fill the given space, consequently destroying any recognizable silhouette and ignoring natural anatomical relationships, the arrangement can be called a *distributive design*. Though it may represent a particular animal and may consist of elements representative of that animal, the requirements of space filling have so distorted it that it is difficult or impossible to identify the abstracted animal or the exact symbolism of the parts (Fig. 8).

It is the purpose of this book to describe some of those stylistic characteristics of Northwest Coast Indian art which have heretofore escaped analysis. None of the principles of representation that have been so well described in the literature will be reviewed, except as they relate directly to organization and form.

6 Woven spruce root hat, Haida. A configurative design of a split wolf is painted around the hat in black, red, and blue-green. Private collection.

7 Woven spruce root hat, Haida. An expansive design representing a beaver is painted in black and red. Private collection.

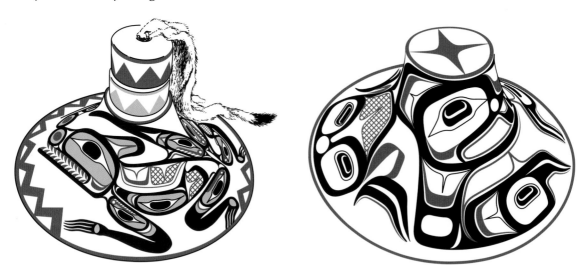

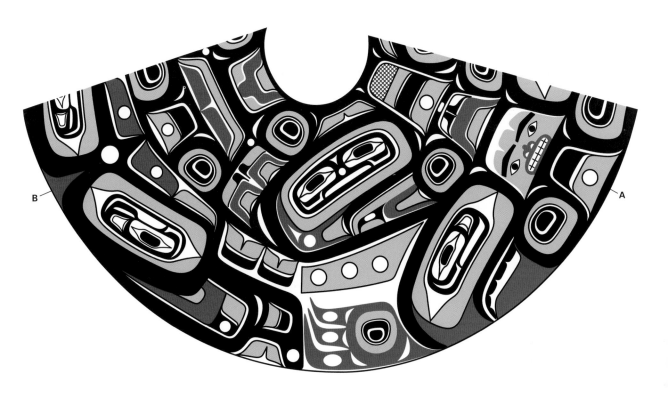

B

A

8 Woven spruce root hat, Tlingit. Slightly more than half the design is shown as if flattened out. The short lines extending from the rims indicate (A) the front and (B) the back of the design. Alaska State Museum II B 830.

IT IS IN THE TWO-DIMENSIONAL ASPECT OF THE "TOTEMIC" art of the Northwest Coast that we can most readily isolate and examine the forms and relationships that typify the art style. The principles that govern two-dimensional design can also be applied to the plastic art of the area; in fact, the two art expressions are so interrelated that it is at times hard to say where one ends and the other begins.

Northwest Coast Indian art is essentially a wooden art. The native trees of the Pacific Coast furnished craftsmen and artists with an abundance of easily worked, highly usable material. Most of the existing examples of art work from this area are wood. Two-dimensional surface decoration on wood was carried out in three ways. Painting was the most common, and possibly the earliest, method. Shallow relief carving, which in effect is two-dimensional and follows exactly the apparent rules for painted design, is a second method of surface treatment. The third technique, which is very often found, is a combination of the other two, that is, relief carving totally or partially painted. A complete listing of all types of wooden objects decorated with one or another of these techniques would be very long and would include boxes, settees, house fronts, interior partitions and screens, canoes (Fig. 9), dishes, spoons, rattles, and many other items. Painting was also used on dressed skins, primarily for ceremonial garments, and basketry. Here the same principles apply as for painting on wood.

Another group of relatively hard materials makes up the bulk of the remainder of Northwest Coast surface-decorated pieces. These materials are (1) metal, mainly copper, silver (Figs. 10 and 58), and gold; (2) bone, horn (Figs. 11A and B and 70), antler, and ivory; and (3) stone, principally the black slate or carbonaceous shale of the Queen Charlotte Islands (Fig. 16). Objects made of these materials are commonly decorated with engraving or shallow relief carving which also conforms to the rules of design that govern painting on wood.

Uses of Two-Dimensional Art

9 Wooden model of a seagoing canoe, Haida. Denver Art Museum 1956.65.

10 Silver bracelets, Haida. Metal engraving was an introduced technique on the Northwest Coast. The white man's gold and silver coins furnished the materials for bracelets and brooches, but the engraved designs frequently represent the best of two-dimensional art. Images cpn09521, cpn09522, cpn09523 (*top to bottom, left*); cpn09519, cpn10005, cpn09513 (*top to bottom, right*) courtesy of Royal B.C. Museum, B.C. Archives.

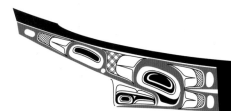

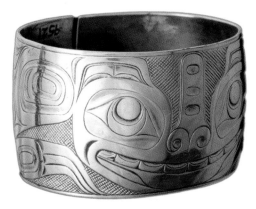

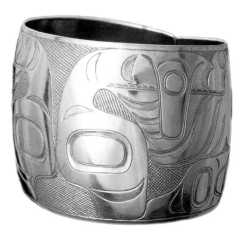

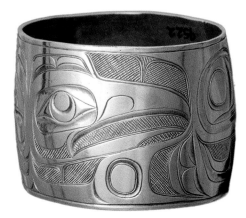

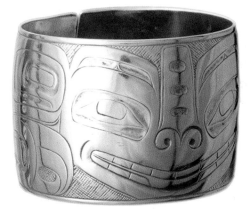

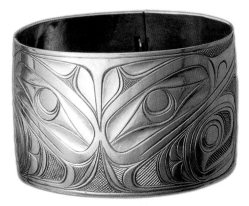

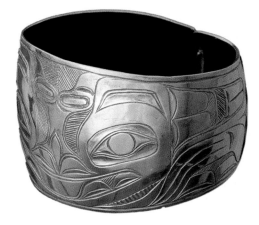

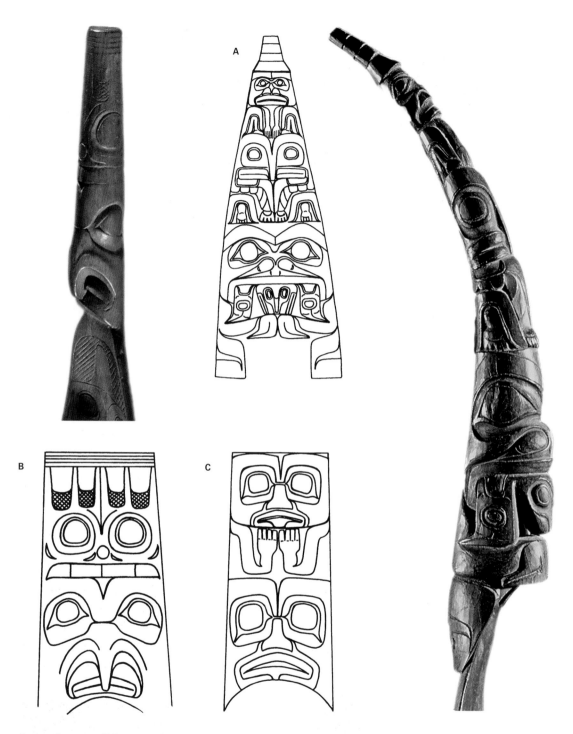

11 Designs "unwrapped" from spoon handles. The close relationship in organization and form between two- and three-dimensional art of the Northwest Coast can be seen in the "unwrapped" designs. Totem poles and other sculptural objects show the same relationship to a greater or lesser degree. A and B, private collection. C, Portland Art Museum 3277.

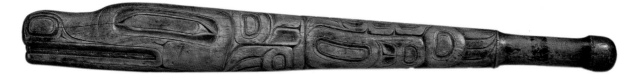

12 Wooden club, Tlingit. The parts of the sea lion represented in this carved club have their conventional two-dimensional form and are organized as a typical two-dimensional design. Unknown Tlingit artist, late nineteenth century, Denver Art Museum Collection: museum purchase from the University of Washington, 1953.603. Photograph © Denver Art Museum.

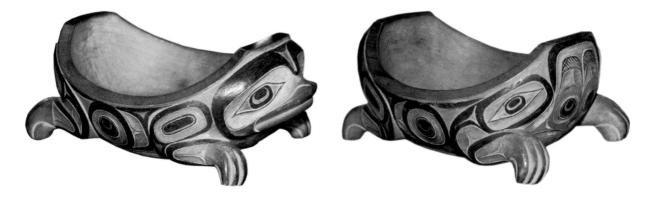

13 Wooden bowl, Haida. The interrelation of two-dimensional design with sculptural form is well illustrated in this frog bowl by the master Haida carver, Charles Edensaw. University of British Columbia Museum of Anthropology A7054.

Many of the objects whose surface decoration can be considered two-dimensional are themselves plastic and sculptural. A painted skin blanket, when it is worn, takes on a new dimension of depth, and the relationship between it and certain carved poles, especially some of those of the Bella Coola, becomes apparent.

Carved gambling sticks, seen together with diagrams of their "unwrapped" designs, suggest even more graphically the degree to which certain Northwest Coast sculptures conform in organization to the principles of painting and relief carving (Willett, 1961:Pl. D and Fig. 1). These gambling sticks are actually wrapped with two-dimensional designs, but the resemblance of some of the finished sticks, carved and cylindrical, to Haida totem poles is striking. The same relationship can be seen in some spoon handles and other small cylindrical objects (Figs. 11 and 12).

Krickeberg (1925:144) describes and illustrates a pair of Haida skin dance leggings with the painted design of a whale in which the tail of the whale forms a skin flap over the foot of the dancer and to which a wooden dorsal fin is sewn, a feature which he describes as "a characteristic shading [*Hinüberspielen*] of surface art into plas-

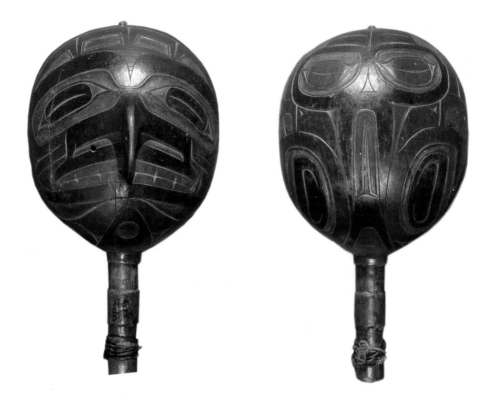

tic art which can sometimes be observed in Northwest art." The Northwest Coast artist moved easily back and forth between two- and three-dimensional work (Fig. 13). Of the four hundred pieces analyzed in the present study, fifty exhibit an easy transition from flat painting or low relief to full sculptural form. Quite frequently the nose, beak, or snout of the creature represented is brought out from the surface of the decorated object, while the rest of the face and body is conventionally flattened and spread over the remaining space (Fig. 14).

Carved wooden rattles, themselves sculptural, are commonly overlaid with an essentially flat design skillfully related to the globular surface (Fig. 14). Spoon bowls and dishes of mountain sheep horn present further examples of shallow relief carving fitted to a three-dimensional surface. In all such objects the principles of design organization and form that apply to truly flat design are apparent. Typical two-dimensional designs are also used in the surface decoration of masks and carved poles, but in the relationship of the flat design to the sculptured forms significant tribal or areal variations, which will be described more fully in the discussion of style, can be seen.

14 Round rattle. Globular rattles of this type attest to the skill of the northern artists in fitting flat designs to three-dimensional forms. The protruding beak of the hawk or thunderbird is a typical example of three-dimensional intrusion in a flat design. Canadian Museum of History, catalogue number VII X 208. Photograph by Bill Holm.

Two other decorative techniques that are represented in the art work of the Northwest Coast are weaving and appliqué. The first, as it applies to this discussion, is limited to the Chilkat blanket and its related aprons and shirts. The second is represented by dance costume items decorated with cloth-on-cloth appliqué, pearl buttons, dentalia, abalone shell, porcupine quills, and glass beads. Of these the cloth, pearl buttons, and glass beads are certainly introduced materials, and to a lesser degree the same could be said of the others, since quillwork was a technique very likely borrowed from the interior in fairly recent times, and extensive use of green abalone shell seems to date only from the period of trade, via the white man's sailing ship, with California, the Pacific islands, and Japan (Heizer, 1940; Leechman, 1942:159–62; and statements by Kwakiutl informants to the author). The pale native abalone was probably used in precontact times, although less extensively, and the use of dentalia is probably very ancient. The conservative character of the Northwest Coast artist is seen, however, in the use of the introduced materials. With all his ingenuity and virtuosity, he retained the essential character of the art style and successfully transferred his principles of design from the old media to the new.

Considering that the vast bulk of Northwest Coast art work existing in museum collections today was produced in the period from 1850 to the first decade of the present century, the creative activity from which it resulted is astounding. Claude Levi-Strauss was probably high in his estimate of the population of the entire Northwest Coast, let alone the northern tribes, considered here, when he wrote:

> At the most flourishing period the tribes of the Northwest Coast totaled one hundred to one hundred and fifty thousand souls, a derisive total when one ponders the intensity of expression and decisive lessons of an art wholly elaborated in this far province of the new world by a population whose density varied, according to the section, from 0.1 to 0.6 inhabitants per square kilometer [Levi-Strauss, 1943:179].

It is difficult to understand how these Indian artists, scattered among the inlets of the rugged northern coast, mastered the complexities of the design system to such a degree that only an occasional piece in the vast museum collections of today deviates from that system. Yet almost every specimen is unique, further attesting to the virtuosity of the native artists, who were able to achieve originality within the framework of rigidly observed rules.

Style

Aside from the symbolic aspect, this is essentially an applied and decorative art. The purely decorative motive applies to a large segment of Indian art of the Northwest Coast, in spite of its underlying function of crest display. That the display characteristic tended to conventionalize the symbolism is no doubt true. But conventionalization, especially at the center of impetus of this art, goes beyond display to such formal organization and reorganization of the crest design as to subordinate the original meaning. "When the purely decorative tendency prevails we have essentially geometrical, highly conventionalized forms, when the idea of representation prevails, we have, on the contrary, more realistic forms" (Boas, 1927:354).

Tribal Variations

At the center of development of Northwest Coast Indian art we have the Haida of the Queen Charlotte Islands and the Coast Tsimshian. Among the artists of these tribes the principles of organization and form suggested below had their greatest development and their most rigid adherence. The decorative tendency prevailed to a large degree, and the highly formalized box and blanket designs seem to have their origin here. Krickeberg (1925:148) believed that the technique of weaving furthered the schematization of form among the Tsimshian, traditional originators of Chilkat-type weaving. Although highly conventionalized decorative design occurs all along the coast, to the south and north of this center the representational motive becomes progressively stronger. Krickeberg (1925:144) characterizes this as a fresh naturalism to the south among the Kwakiutl, Nootka, and Salish and a certain relationship to Eskimo engraving and painting among the Tlingit to the north. The shift in emphasis is gradual—Bella Bella art, for example, has a close affinity to its Coast Tsimshian counterpart. Two-dimensional art of all these groups, however, is much more closely related than is their sculpture, especially among the northern tribes of Tlingit, Haida, Tsimshian, and Bella Bella. It appears to be impossible to differentiate with certainty, on the basis of style alone, two-dimensional design of these four northern tribes, since both decorative

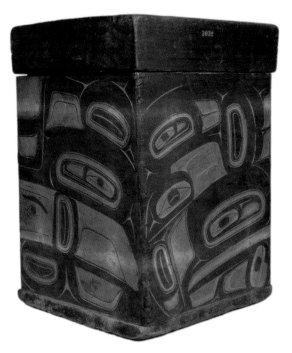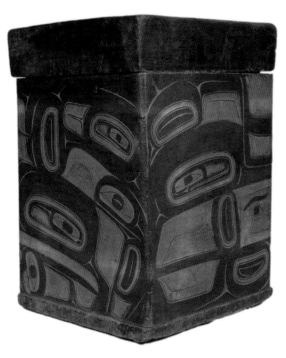

15 Carved and painted box, Haida. The formlines are so massive, and the arrangement of elements is so compact, that ground is reduced to thin lines and slits. It is in this type of design that the primary formlines may most easily be mistaken for the background, with a resulting misunderstanding of their function and form. Canadian Museum of History, catalogue number VII B 139, image numbers S86-1680, S86-1681.

and representative tendencies occur in the work of all, and the conventions of the art are so strong throughout this area. It cannot be doubted that there are tribal variations, but on the basis of present knowledge they are not apparent.

Unfortunately, museum records are not always reliable when it comes to establishing the provenience of a given piece. Often, of course, the object was collected casually and many years later acquired from the heirs of the collector, with only vague identification or none at all. In some cases a staff member has furnished an identification, without qualifying it, for the catalogue on the basis of his knowledge of tribal styles. When this "educated guess" is wide of the mark it is easily detected by the student, but the knowledge that this kind of cataloguing has taken place casts doubt on other identifications that may or may not be more accurate. Sometimes the researcher may uncover more information in further checking of the documents related to the collection. For example, a bracelet included in this study, which is catalogued as Tsimshian, was described by G. T. Emmons, the collector, in his collection notes as "smaller and beautifully carved silver-bracelet found in Victoria, B.C. but the work of the Tsimshean or Haida of the Northern Coast in design and workmanship." Emmons was notoriously meticulous in his collection notes, and they are well worth study. Although he collected the beautifully carved and painted chest now in the Washington State Museum from the Chilkat at Klukwan (Fig. 54 and Inverarity, 1950:Fig. 25), he stated that it had not been made by them, but had been obtained from the Haida. On the other hand, a similar chest, obviously from the north, in the National Museum of Canada was collected from the Saanich of southern Vancouver Island and in the absence of qualifying information is so catalogued.

To compound the difficulty of identification, there seems to be as great a variation among the styles of the artists of any one of these northern tribes as is discernible between "tribal" styles themselves. Some Haida work shows a tendency to a heavy angularity of line and a certain compact arrangement of elements (Fig. 15). Very different is the open, freely curvilinear style exemplified by the work of Charles Edensaw or the somewhat delicate, attenuated design with long tapering U forms and multiangled composition seen in certain Haida slate pieces and paintings (Fig. 16).

The origin of the hat shown in Figure 6 has been unknown, but I have long considered it to be a Tlingit piece on the basis of the general similarity of the painting, in concept and detail, to some known Tlingit specimens. On the basis of a comparison with a sketchbook of drawings made for Dr. Newcombe by Tom Price of Ninstints, it

16 Argillite platter, Haida. This slate or argillite platter with a man emerging from a salmon carved in high relief in the center illustrates the narrow elements and multiangled arrangement characteristic of the work of some Haida artists. Attributed to John Cross. Image courtesy of the Seattle Art Museum, 91.1.73. Gift of John H. Hauberg.

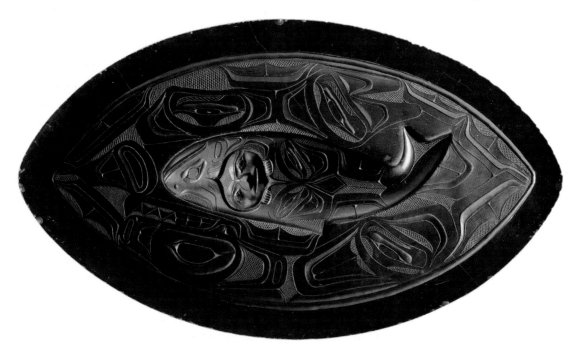

now appears definitely to be the work of that Haida artist. Wilson Duff and John Sendey of the Provincial Museum of British Columbia, which owns the Newcombe drawings, have concurred in assigning the hat painting to Tom Price.

The hat painting in Figure 7 is also Haida, possibly by Charles Edensaw, but is very different in concept, conforming more nearly to what we might think of as a "typical" Haida design. Edensaw himself has been called an "individualist" and an "innovator" in his approach to art. His work, however, conforms entirely to the system of precepts described below. It seems that every Haida artist of any consequence was an innovator, and each developed his own distinctive handling of form and space within the prescribed system.

Decoration of Masks and Totem Poles

In the two-dimensional surface decoration of masks and carved poles much more apparent tribal variations exist. Among all groups the significant features of the face—eyebrows, eyes, nostrils, and lips—are painted on masks and on the faces of figures on carved poles in a relatively uniform manner. Tribal differences are slight and become noticeable only at a great distance from the art center. In the north, among the Tlingit, Haida, and Tsimshian, any other surface decoration on masks is often applied with a minimum of relationship to the sculptured forms. In concept such painting is used like the face painting of the north (Boas, 1900: 13–24; Swanton, 1908:xlviii–lvi): flat realistic or conventionalized designs are applied with seeming disregard for the structure of the face (Fig. 17A). In the south, particularly among the Kwakiutl, the painted forms emphasize, accent, and conform to the sculptural forms (Fig. 17C). Midway between these extremes are the Bella Coola, whose masks are often painted with large areas of flat color that deliberately cross the carved forms (Fig. 17B). If a generalization could be made, it might be that mask painting in the north is independent of the structural form; among the Bella Coola it opposes the structural form; and among the Kwakiutl it coincides with the structural form.

In large carvings and poles the painting of faces is treated in much the same manner as in masks. In the handling of two-dimensional surface decoration of the remainder of the sculpture other variations appear. Among all groups it seems standard procedure to treat large flat areas such as wings, tails, and ears as two-dimensional and to organize the decoration on these parts in much the same way as

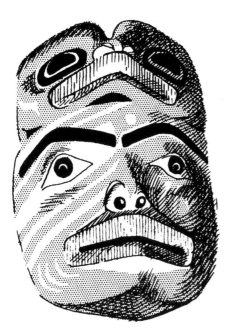

A

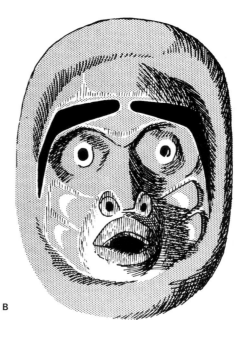

B

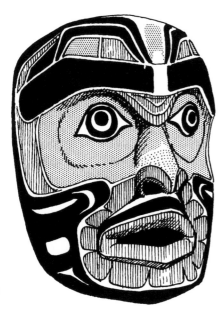

C

17 (A) Face mask, Tlingit. The asymmetrical pattern is placed apparently without regard for the form or features of the face. It is painted in light blue-green, a color commonly seen in Tlingit specimens. Statens Etnografiska Museum, Stockholm 00.32.8. (B) Face mask, Bella Coola. Thin points of contrasting color crossing the form, such as those in vermilion on the blue forehead of this mask, are typical of Bella Coola painting. Statens Etnografiska Museum, Stockholm 04.19.2. (C) Face mask, Kwakiutl. A strong pattern of black, red, green, and sometimes white, coinciding with the carved form of the mask, is characteristic of southern Kwakiutl mask painting. Burke Museum catalogue number 1-1634.

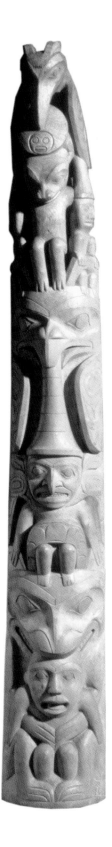

the corresponding part of a flat painting (Fig. 18). Kwakiutl commonly extend such painting over much of the surface of the pole, integrating it with the three-dimensional form, as in the carved faces and masks.

Tribal distinctions in carving style (Wingert, 1951:73–94) are not within the scope of this study except as they are directly related to two-dimensional design. In this respect it is interesting to note that the total organization of sculptured columns of some groups, especially the Haida and Bella Coola, falls readily into the frame of organization for two-dimensional design. Poles of these two tribes are often organized as flat designs wrapped around a semicylindrical surface: the Haida poles then deeply and boldly carved, the Bella Coola shallowly, as a low relief, but each element containing such a convexity as to give the whole carving a voluminous, almost bulging, effect.

18 Model totem pole, Haida. Typical two-dimensional handling of the wings of the creatures represented can be seen. Charles Edensaw. The Field Museum 18216.

Color

In the use of color we find one of the great unifying characteristics of the art. The colors in painting were limited, before the opening of the trade with Europeans, to a few natural pigments. The conventions of the art were so strong, or the Indian artists so conservative, that the introduction of trade paints did not materially affect the selection and use of color. The principal colors were black, red, and green, blue, or blue-green. The black was generally derived from lignite, although graphite and charcoal were also used. Red, before the trade period, was derived from ochers, and several specimens of paint stone in the Washington State Museum have been identified as hematite. Mungo Martin, a Kwakiutl trained from youth as an artist, told me that it was his understanding that the Kwakiutl had "no good red, only brown like iron rust," until the Hudson's Bay Company introduced "China red in paper packages." This would agree with Emmons' statement in reference to Chilkat face painting: "The primitive colors were black, from powdered charcoal, and red, from pulverized ocher, but after the advent of Europeans, vermilion of commerce took the place of the duller mineral red" (Emmons, 1916:16–17). The "vermilion of commerce" is Chinese vermilion, which was packaged in paper envelopes. Native cinnabar may have furnished red pigment also, but the purity and richness of the vermilion coloring on a large proportion of Indian painted objects suggest the Chinese vermilion.

The greens and blue-greens were probably derived from copper minerals. Shotridge identifies a greenish-blue pigment used on an old helmet as "the covelline, a sulphide of copper" (Shotridge, 1929:339). Among the Bella Coola such extensive use was made of a medium cobalt blue that it might be considered characteristic of the painting of that tribe.

White was occasionally used, as well as yellow. Sometimes the whites of eyes, teeth, and small separating or relieving elements were painted white, and the Kwakiutl commonly used it as a ground color, especially since the last decade of the nineteenth century. The occurrence of white and yellow is, however, so limited in the two-dimensional art of the northern tribes that they can be considered unusual; black, red, and blue-green are therefore considered the standard colors in painting. In the Chilkat blanket and related woven objects the white of the wool (as the ground color) and a yellow derived from wolf moss (*Evernia vulpina*) are typical, along with blue-green and black.

Elements of the Art

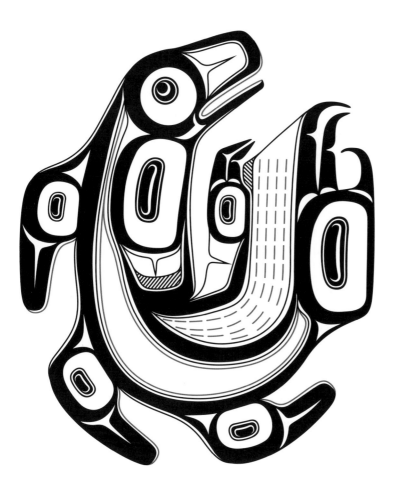

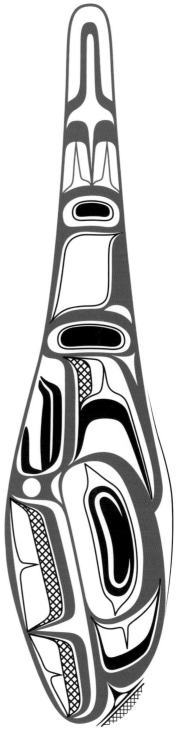

19 Painting from a spruce root mat, Haida. Private collection.

20 Painted wooden spoon, Stikine Tlingit. Burke Museum catalogue number 2334.

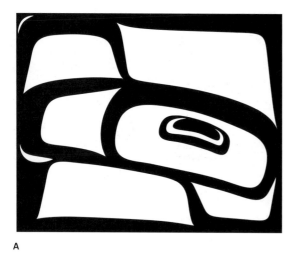

A

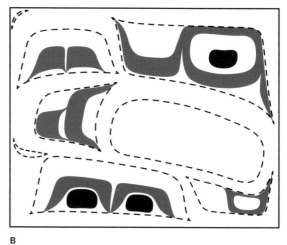

B

Painting was done with brushes of various sizes made of hair, often of the porcupine, inserted in a handle of wood. The bristles were fastened in a flat bundle cut off at an angle on the end. The brush was drawn toward the painter, edgeways for lines, flatways for filling in areas. Mungo Martin stated that the handle should be round and slim so that the painter could twirl it easily between thumb and forefinger in order to turn corners, in a manner suggesting the technique of a modern sign painter. The pigment was mixed with a medium prepared by chewing dried salmon eggs wrapped in cedar bark and spitting the saliva and egg oil mixture into the paint dish (Boas, 1909:403). Leechman (1932:37–42) attributes some paint properties to the cedar bark; the personal experience of the writer indicates that the use of cedar bark wrapping for the eggs serves primarily to retain the membranous parts and keep them out of the paint itself.

Emmons (1907:350) established that there was a standardized system for the placement of the several colors of a Chilkat blanket which guided the weaver, even though the pattern board used gave no intimation of their position, except for the black. The literature does not note that there was a similar system, if anything more rigid, which applied to two-dimensional painted art. This system is all the more interesting because it gives us a clue to the thinking of the Indian artist in terms of figure and ground. The color arrangement formula was followed with amazing consistency over the whole coast, even including the Kwakiutl, who were late-comers to the system.

21 The three classes of design elements and their relation to color and surface. (A) The black primary formline pattern, forming a continuous grid of relatively even weight and complexity. Inner ovoids are always free-floating. (B) Red secondary elements and formline complexes. Inner ovoids enclosed by secondary ovoids are secondary, although always black. (C) Isolated blue-green tertiary elements filling much of the remaining space. True lines border many of them. (D) The three classes together. (E) Cross section showing relation of color to surface form, when carved. Primary and secondary designs are on the plane surface. Tertiary elements and ground are variously recessed, the former either blue-green or unpainted and the latter unpainted.

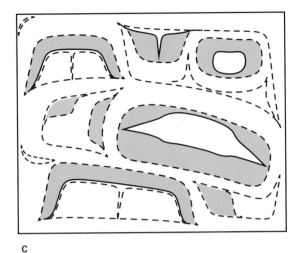

C

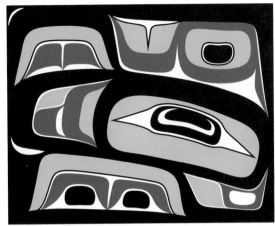

D

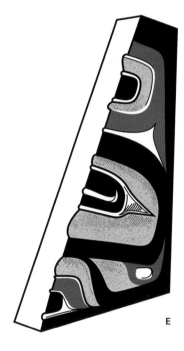

E

Corresponding to the three standard colors are three classes of design elements. Black can be termed the primary color, and the elements painted black can ordinarily be called primary elements (Fig. 19). It is represented in the illustrations as ■.

Red is the color next in importance and will be termed the secondary color. Red elements will be called secondary elements. Red and black can be substituted for each other as primary and secondary elements under certain conditions. Of the painted pieces analyzed, 85 per cent used black for the primary design; 13 per cent used red as primary (Fig. 20); and the remaining 2 per cent used black in some areas and red in others. Red is represented in the illustrations as ■.

Blue-green occupies a special place in the system of color use and will be called the tertiary color ■.

Primary Color Use

The primary color, usually black, is used for the main *formlines* of the design (Fig. 21A). A formline is the characteristic swelling and diminishing linelike figure delineating design units. These formlines merge and divide to make a continuous flowing grid over the whole decorated area, establishing the principal forms of the design. One of the most striking features of the primary design is its continuity. In a typical piece all primary units are connected, with the exception of the inner ovoids of joints and eye designs. It is possible to begin tracing the primary forms at any point and to touch them all, with the exception noted, without a break. A few examples show breaks between large primary complexes, but only one of the examples recorded showed a real lack of continuity. A few other pieces show almost no primary continuity, but were so atypical in other respects that recording was impossible with the check list used (Barbeau, 1953:Fig. 185; Keithahn, 1962:19 and 1963:134).

There is another very important characteristic of the primary design. If the design is carved in low relief, the primary formlines are without exception on the plane surface of the carved material (Fig. 21E).

Secondary Color Use

The secondary color, usually red, is used in formlines of secondary importance to the design, for details, accents, and continuants of primary designs (Fig. 21B). Secondary designs are often enclosed by primary formlines and are always in contact with the adjacent primary units at one or more points. They may occur as isolated single units or as complexes, in which case they exhibit the same continuity to be found in primary design complexes. In every way except color they are like designs of the primary class. They may even enclose "subsecondary" design units of their own.

Red is the usual color for cheeks and tongues; arms, legs, hands, and feet are red in about half of the examples in which they occur. Red can be used as the primary color in all of the design. When it is used in primary elements, black takes its place for the secondary formlines.

There seems to be only one primary element for which red is almost never used. That is the inner ovoid of an eye or joint design, which is almost always black. Of the 269 pieces showing color, 246 used black exclusively for this inner ovoid. Most of the others used black in some of the inner ovoids and red, blue, natural, or inlay of copper or abalone in others. Probably significant is the fact that of the eleven pieces using only red for the inner ovoid, eight were dishes of the type shown in Figure 52A, and four of those were documented as having been collected in the Haida village of Massett between 1887 and 1889. Another exception is in the case of the design appearing on a black ground, in which event the inner ovoid is red, as a primary element. An example of this usage is seen in appliqué blankets and dance shirts, which are typically dark blue with the design in red.

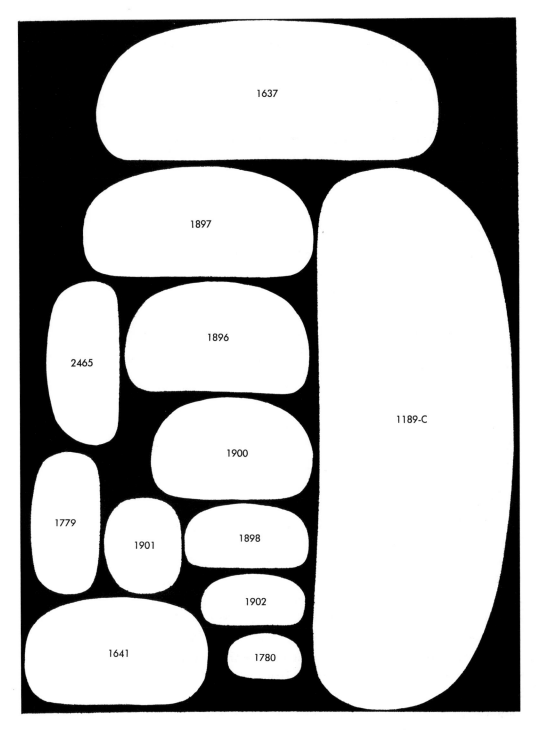

1637

1897

1189-C

2465

1896

1900

1779

1901

1898

1902

1641

1780

22 Tracings of ovoid templates. Burke Museum.

Secondary elements also appear only on the plane surface of relief carvings (Fig. 21E). It is fairly common to find red on the convex surfaces of tongues and limbs of the represented creature, as these parts are often shown in high relief, and in these cases the curved surface plane corresponds to the flat surface of the rest of the decorated area. Only 1 specimen, of 105 employing red on a carved surface, showed that color on a recessed ground area, and 6 others used red in recessed elements ordinarily considered tertiary.

Tertiary Color Use

Blue-green, blue, or green are the colors used for the elements of the third class (Fig. 21C). Blue-green (as all three colors will be called here) is not always used; when it is absent the tertiary elements are left unpainted, producing the effect of ground or negative space. It is not always certain which of the blue-green areas really represent ground and which can be truly considered positive tertiary elements. I have come to consider an enclosed blue-green painted area to be tertiary. There are many characteristic elements that are always tertiary and are easily recognized as such. They include the eye socket, or space between the inner and outer ovoids of eye or joint design; some solid U's; split U's; and certain spaces between primary and secondary designs in ears, feathers, teeth and mouth, fins, and other related fillers. They are always enclosed by primary or secondary elements, and are isolated, seldom (i.e., 16/400) forming tertiary complexes, as do primary and secondary elements.

A most significant practice in the use of the tertiary color occurs on painted relief carving where it always appears on areas recessed below the plane surface (Fig. 21E). Of the painted and carved specimens, very few (2/109) show any deviation. In uncarved paintings without the blue-green there may be a tertiary significance to narrow black or red true lines bordering all or part of an unpainted area.

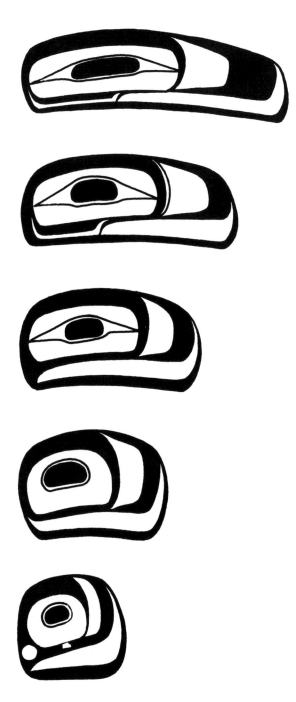

23 "Salmon-trout's-head" elaboration of inner ovoids. The adjustment of design unit proportion to fit space requirements is illustrated by these ovoid examples from various painted boxes.

Perhaps this line is a representation of the rim of the shallowly hollowed element. Visually, it does work in this way. A very interesting and perhaps highly significant example of this use of line to define a tertiary design unit is to be seen in a carved and painted box in the Alaska State Museum (No. 11B 799), in which a typical tertiary unit on one face of the box is concave, while its counterpart on the adjacent side is left flat and outlined in black.

Since, in relief carvings, primary and secondary elements are on the flat surface and tertiary units and ground are recessed, it is entirely practical to paint the primary-secondary pattern before beginning any carving. In fact, numerous experiments by the writer with both methods have shown that painting before carving is faster than carving before painting, is less likely to result in improperly proportioned formlines, allows finer adjustments of form, and facilitates the distribution of design weight. Two characteristics, seen in the few specimens examined with the question of painting-carving sequence in mind, point to the possibility that this sequence was followed, at least some of the time. First, no red or black paint was found in grooves or on the edges of recessed areas where it would surely have sometimes run if painting had followed carving, especially since in some cases the painted form actually crossed the carved grooves intended to define it. Then, certain incised lines bordering formlines were incomplete, especially at the tapering ends of U complexes, where several such lines converge. This would seem to be unlikely if the forms had been defined by carving before painting.

Certainly the formline structure of the art is more natural to painting than to carving. Formlines, the fundamental elements of the art, are always uncarved and are outlined by carving. Were this basically a carved art it would seem that the most important elements would be modeled, rather than the reverse. Similarly, a true line is not represented in carving by a groove, but by a pair of grooves bordering a narrow flat surface.

A more thorough examination of many more pieces with this problem in mind is needed before more objective conclusions can be drawn.

In the following descriptions of various design units the class or classes to which each belongs will be mentioned.

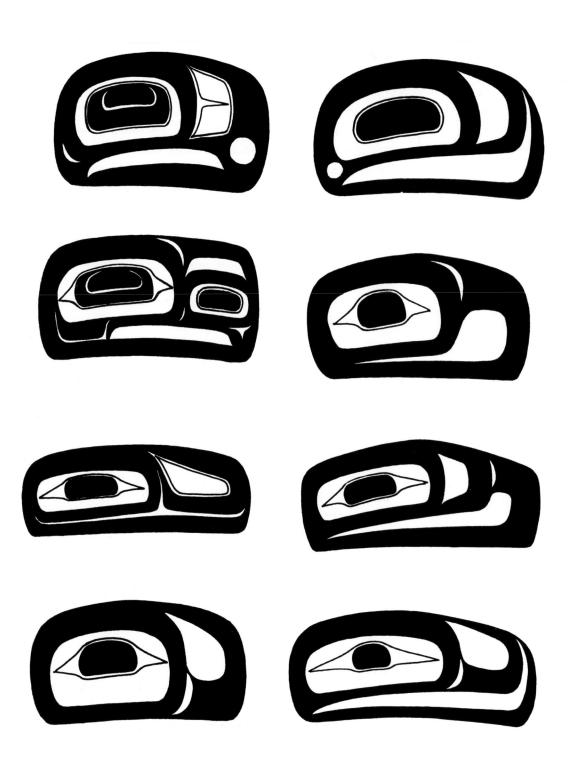

24 Inner ovoid elaborations. Fig. 39 diagrams the construction of the typical "salmon-trout's-head" form of the inner ovoid. Here are seen some of the many possible variations on this theme. Canadian Museum of History.

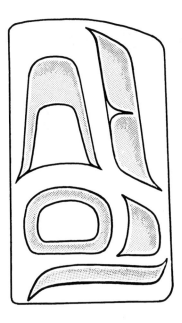

25 Totem pole detail, Haida. The design represents the flipper of a whale and shows the flipper attached directly to the "salmon-trout's-head" joint. University of British Columbia Museum of Anthropology.

Form

The Formline

One of the most characteristic features of Northwest Coast art is the use of the formline. To call it line only would be to minimize its importance as a formal element. The constantly varying width of the formline gives the design a calligraphic character, and one is tempted to assume that this was achieved by varying the direction of the brush as a modern sign writer manipulates his one-stroke brush. A careful examination of Indian paintings reveals, however, that the formlines have been outlined and filled in, a method consistent with the well-known use of bark templates and corroborated by Mungo Martin in conversation with the writer. Interestingly, of the hundreds of bark templates seen, none was a pattern of a formline (Figs. 22 and 29). Consequently, when templates have been used, the primary formlines are negative in the sense that they are the spaces between patterns. This gave the artist considerable control over the formlines themselves, but he had always to hold uppermost the concept that they were, in the end, the positive delineating force of the painting, and that they must also conform to somewhat rigid characteristics.

Formlines swell and diminish, rarely retaining the same width for any distance. Generally they swell in the center of a given design unit and diminish at the ends. The width of a formline usually changes with a major change of direction. These changes of width are governed by the specific design unit formed and its relation to adjacent units.

Formlines are essentially curvilinear. The curves are gentle and sweeping, breaking suddenly into sharper semiangular curves and, immediately upon completing the necessary direction change (usually around 90 degrees), straightening to a gentle curve again.

Ovoids

The most characteristic single design unit in the art is the formline ovoid used as eyes, joints, and various space fillers (Fig. 22). It has been variously termed a rounded rectangle, an angular oval, a bean-shaped figure, and other more or less descriptive names. Although the term ovoid is no more accurate than these others, it is short and handy and will be used herein to signify this design unit. Swan (1874:5 and Fig. 12), in 1874, gave an interesting Haida account of

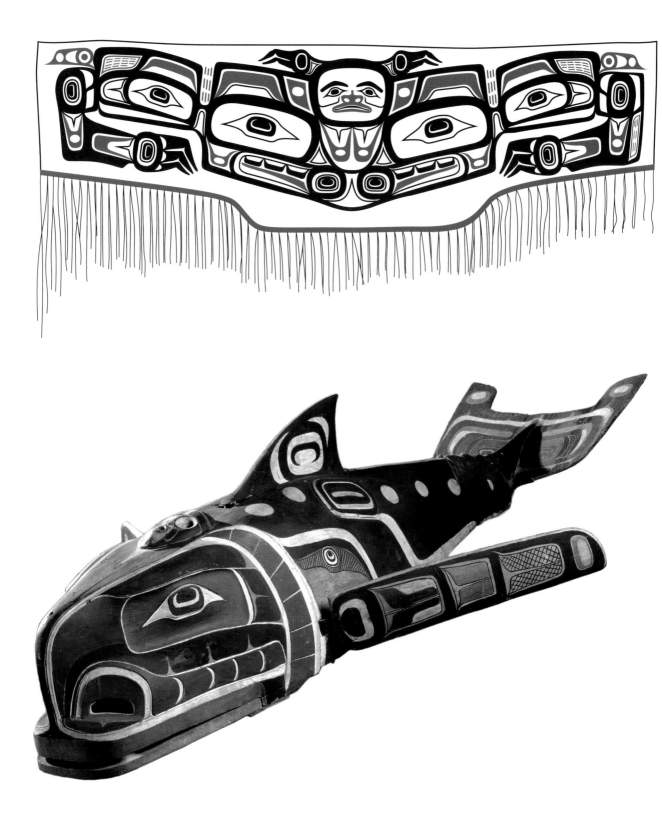

26 Painted skin kilt. Private collection.

the origin of this design, linking it to the elliptical spots to be seen on either side of the body of a young skate. The ovoid takes a very specific form which can, however, be varied in proportion. In each case the individual elements of the design unit enclosed in the ovoid are proportionately lengthened or shortened to fit and preserve the varying width of the tertiary space (Fig. 23).

An ovoid is always convex on its upper side and at its ends. If it appears concave on the upper side it is upside down, and, if it represents an eye, the head of the creature of which it is a part can be considered to be upside down. Joints may be shown either way, depending upon the space-filling requirements.

The lower side is usually concave, but with less curvature than the upper side so as to retain the greatest width in the center. In general the shorter the ovoid the less concave the lower side, until in extremely short forms the lower edge may even be convex. In such cases the ovoid may actually be a circle. The formline is widest on the upper side, tapering slightly at the upper corners, then diminishing further to the lower corners, and sometimes swelling slightly to the middle of the lower side. The swell of the lower side is not pronounced enough to prevent the enclosed shape from having its greatest width at the center. The ovoid is invariably horizontally symmetrical, and ovoid templates are often made by folding the bark down the middle before cutting. This symmetry is not so apparent on the outer edge of the formline ovoid as it is usually modified by contact with other design units.

The corners of ovoids are points of tension, as are all formline corners. Junctures with other forms and with formlines usually take place near the corners. Elaboration of the form due to the presence of transitional devices takes place at the corners. The lower corners, because of the rather sudden change from convexity to concavity, are most angular and hence the points of greatest tension. In practice an ovoid, except for the inner ovoid of eye or joint designs, is practically never free-floating, but is attached to other formlines at one or more points. Most of the exceptions are in relatively modern pieces, such as those atypical paintings mentioned in the discussion of continuity in primary design. There are very few exceptions to the rule that inner ovoids are free-floating. A few northern examples show joints in the form of the "salmon-trout's-head" ovoid attached directly to adjacent forms (Figs. 25 and 26). Although this is not the usual procedure, the elaborated ovoid may be considered analogous

27 Whale mask, Kwakiutl. Although the decoration of the fins and tail of this southern Kwakiutl whale mask is more like northern painting than many Kwakiutl examples, it differs from the northern style in several respects. Freer use of color, appearance of design units not found in northern work (especially in the secondary-tertiary fillers of primary formline U's), less formline continuity, and the frequent use of inner ovoids attached to adjacent design units are some of the more obvious points of difference. Unknown Kwakwaka'wakw artist, 1900, Denver Art Museum Collection: Museum Purchase from the University of Washington, 1953.404. Photograph © Denver Art Museum.

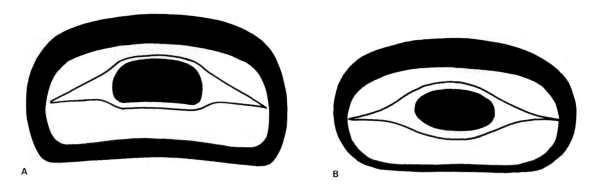

A   B

28 (A) Characteristic firm ovoid and eyelid. (B) Soft ovoids and eyelid, not typical of old specimens.

to the similarly organized face designs, which are not free-floating. There are numerous southern Kwakiutl specimens with joints identical to typical inner ovoids, attached directly to adjacent units, one of the ways in which the Kwakiutl version of two-dimensional art differs from its northern counterpart (Fig. 27).

Eyelids

Closely associated with the ovoid and as characteristic of this art is the eyelid shape. It is familiar to anyone who has ever looked at an example of Northwest Coast Indian art as a somewhat lenticular shape, rounded in the center, pointed at the ends, and enclosing a round or oval spot suggesting the iris of an eye (Fig. 28A). It is not surprising that the shape of this eyelid unit follows fixed rules. The length and width of the unit are in proportion to the enclosing ovoid, that is, eyelids within a short ovoid are short and wide; those within a long ovoid are long and narrow. The shape of the eye seems to be determined to some degree by the type of creature represented, and this also affects the shape of the surrounding ovoid or eye socket. The rule for the shape of the eyelid is as follows. The line forming the lids follows closely along the upper and lower sides of the enclosed ovoid (iris). At the corners it breaks, or curves more sharply inward. Since the outer corners of the eyelid are slightly below its center, the lines extending from the upper breaks to the outer corners are almost straight, while the lines connecting the lower breaks with the outer corners may be slightly concave. The lower curve typically breaks at the corners of the inner, or iris, ovoid and then quickly breaks again in a reverse curve, from which it proceeds in a nearly straight line to the outer corners. These curves are not completely smooth but show definite directional changes at the points indicated. It is this firm handling of curves which gives the

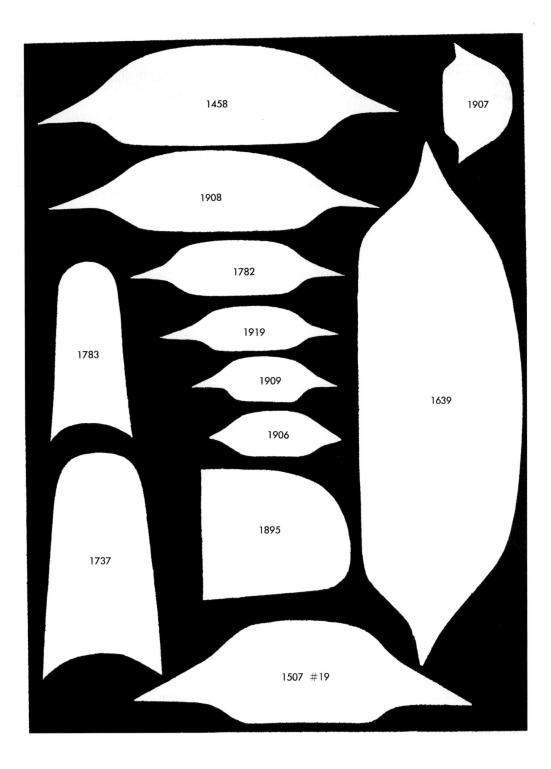

29 Tracings of eyelid and U templates.
Burke Museum.

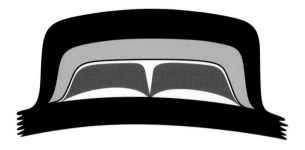

best Northwest Coast work such surety and force, and the lack of it which so often brands the work of copyists of Indian design (Fig. 28B).

The whole eyelid unit is placed above the center of the surrounding tertiary space, and often the eyelid line is drawn closer to the iris ovoid at the top than at the bottom. This illustrates an important principle of the art which can be termed *nonconcentricity* and which will be discussed more fully in the section on "principles."

The iris ovoid is almost without exception black, and the eyelid line is generally black also, although a few red examples have been noted. Elaborations of the ovoid, such as the "salmon-trout's-head" and the "double-eye" are also black.

U Forms

The U form and its variants are as characteristic as the ovoid. U forms result when both ends of a formline turn in the same direction and each tapers to a point at their inevitable juncture with another formline. They can be very long, thin, featherlike figures or wide, solid forms enclosing little or no negative or tertiary space. They occur in all three design classes, often one within the other. Typically the U form is thick on the end and thinner on the sides or legs. In the primary form the legs of the U have thickness comparable to that of other formlines in the design. Secondary and subsecondary U's may have legs as thin as true line, in which case the wide end of the U may be cross-hatched rather than solidly painted, depending on the requirements of design weight and detail. The legs may be of almost any length, or they may be nearly eliminated and the U form solidly colored. A single specimen may show a bewildering variety of primary, secondary, and tertiary U's. Solid secondary U's are often arranged in pairs within another

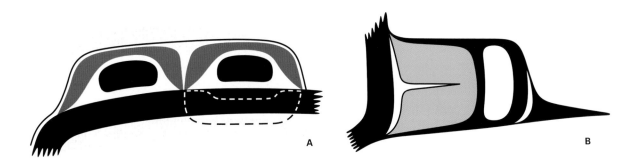

31 (A) Eye U. The dotted lines indicate the origin of the design. (B) Split U within a primary U with a negative ovoid relief and pointed extension.

formline U, frequently separated from it by a tertiary element also of U form (Fig. 30).

A peculiar form is occasionally seen (21/400) which seems to violate the rules since the end of the U is narrower than its sides and it encloses an ovoid. This ovoid is a clue to the unusual shape of the U. Examination shows that this U form is derived from the tertiary space above the upper eyelid line in a typical eye design; a tertiary modified into a secondary unit—the only case where the inner ovoid has no outline, attesting to the tertiary function of true line (Fig. 31A).

If the closed end of the U is very thick it may be relieved with a negative ovoid. It is sometimes further elaborated with a point which is an extension of one of the sides and is relieved at its juncture with the end of the U by one of a group of transitional devices (Fig. 31B).

There is a variety of tertiary U forms. Commonly the space enclosed in a typical primary or secondary U may be recessed, painted blue-green, outlined, or all three, as a tertiary unit. Very often a solid tertiary U is separated from the formline at its base by a narrow, crescent-shaped space. This kind of separating space and others related to it occur frequently and will be treated more fully under the heading of "Transitional Devices."

The tertiary split U, elaborated with a "pointed double curve, like a brace" (Boas in Emmons, 1907:371), which nearly splits the unit into two parts, also occurs frequently (272/400). It, like the closely related solid U, is typically enclosed by a primary or secondary formline U and may be either merely outlined, outlined and hatched in black or red, or solidly painted blue. There is also a primary-secondary version of the split U, but it is always red or black, never blue-green, and always on the plane surface, never recessed. It is much

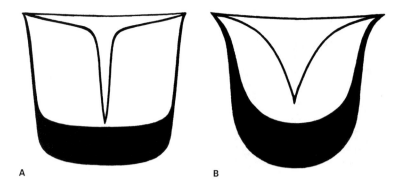

A   B   C

less common than the tertiary split U (50/400). Very infrequently a red-painted, although otherwise typical, tertiary split U appears (15/400). Some of these are in the ears of carved figures and may relate in color to the naturalistically carved ears in some masks which are typically painted red.

Some split U designs show an even curve from the corner of the base to the apex of the split. Most split U's, and especially those in specimens of fine workmanship, show a strong break in the curve at the base of the split, which itself is narrow and nearly straight-sided (Fig. 32A). On flat paintings the split itself is done in red or black line, and even in designs that are both carved and painted with blue-green split U's, the split may be outlined in black or occasionally red. The outer edge of the split U unit, in flat paintings, may also be shown in a line of the same color as the split (Fig. 32C). Frequently, however, the unit is defined by the inner edge of the enclosing primary or secondary formline. This seems to be the rule if the enclosing formline U is hatched rather than solidly painted. Split U's with and without outlines are found in the same paintings. Their use appears to have been left to the discretion of the artist, probably depending upon the need for elaboration in the area of the painting involved. The split makes the U design look something like a feather, and it is an important element in feather designs. It, like all other U forms, is never free-floating, but is always joined at the base to a formline.

Other Tertiary Units

Since tertiary units are, in the main, fillers between primary and secondary formlines, they assume many forms. Most common are the solid tertiary U's and the closely related split U's already described. Of frequent occurrence is the tertiary U separating a primary form-

32 (A) Typical U complex with semi-angular curves. (B) U complex with soft curves, not characteristic of old Northwest Coast designs. (C) Split U with outline.

33 Tertiary S enclosed by primary and secondary complexes.

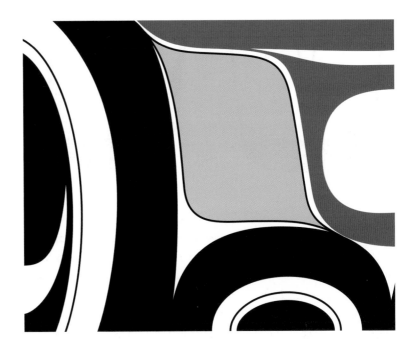

line U and the enclosed secondary or pair of secondary solid U's (Fig. 30). This tertiary U differs in form from the usual primary and secondary formline U in that its thickness is nearly constant from one end to the other. As in the case of other tertiary units in flat paintings, it is outlined in red or black. In relief carvings it is recessed and, if painted, is blue-green.

Often the tertiary space left between primary and secondary units or complexes takes an S shape, or a nearly rectangular form, with one pair of diagonal corners rounded and the other pair pointed (Fig. 33). Another relatively common tertiary unit is a modified U separating primary and enclosed secondary U's in an area which tapers to one end to the extent that one leg of the tertiary U is eliminated, giving it an L-like form (Fig. 34). There are occasions when the usable space between primary and secondary formlines assumes a more complex shape, but the tertiary unit enclosed is rarely elaborated beyond those described.

Eyebrows

Eyebrows occur in stylized faces where the eye sockets are not defined by ovoid formlines. These faces are somewhat realistic and are readily recognized as faces, although they are often symbolic of bodies, joints, or other body parts in more abstract designs (Fig. 35A).

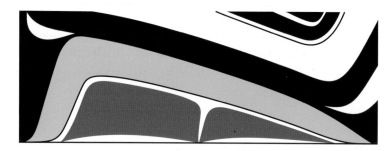

34 Tertiary L enclosing secondary double U's in a tapering space.

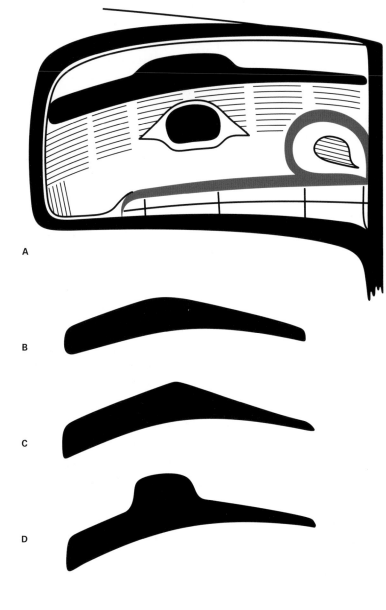

35 (A) Stylized face with eyebrow, from a painted box. (B) Rounded eyebrow. (C) Angular eyebrow. (D) Eyebrow with hump.

A

B

C

D

Typically the eyebrows are curved much like the upper side of an ovoid. They are widest near or just outside the center and taper toward the ends, the inner end usually being considerably narrower (Fig. 35B and C). Sometimes there is a pronounced hump on the upper edge at the point of greatest width. The outline of this hump takes the form of the upper edge of a typical ovoid (Fig. 35A and D).

Primary and Secondary Formlines Defining a Single Form

In certain cases a space is defined by a combination of primary and secondary formlines. The most common example of this usage is in the definition of the main eye socket space in large animal faces, especially on chests and boxes. Here the primary formline becomes in turn the line of the lower jaw (Fig. 36A), the outside of the face (Fig. 36B), then the upper and interorbital border of the eye socket (Fig. 36C and D), and about one half of the lower border (Fig 36E), where it breaks downward and makes a tapering juncture with the lower jaw (Fig. 36F), thus forming the corner of the mouth. The outer lower corner of the eye socket ovoid is defined by a secondary cheek design (Figs. 36G, 41, and 42). This secondary cheek design occurs even in some sculptural faces, usually in a simple form (Fig. 37).

Usually, in one of the two main decorated sides of a chest or box the central face is handled in a slightly more elaborate fashion, possibly with symbolic significance (Fig. 38). The eye socket is long and narrow, and the primary formline, instead of continuing along the inside and lower border of the eye socket ovoid, merely dips in a V (Fig. 38A) and continues as the upper border of the adjacent eye socket. The mouth and nose are formed of another primary complex joining the main formline at the V and at the corners of the mouth (Fig. 38B). The secondary cheek design consequently is elongated along the eye socket and runs smoothly, or "fairs" into the line of the nostril (Figs. 38C and 43). Typically, the long eye socket thus formed encloses a correspondingly long iris ovoid which is often developed into the "double-eye" form. The "double-eye" and the typical "salmon-trout's-head" are organized in exactly the same way as these large faces, with the single exception that the cheek design is primary and black (Fig. 39).

An incomplete Haida drawing in the collection of the Provincial Museum of British Columbia shows clearly that the complete eye socket ovoid was drawn as a unit (using a template) and then the corner of the mouth and the cheek design developed within the

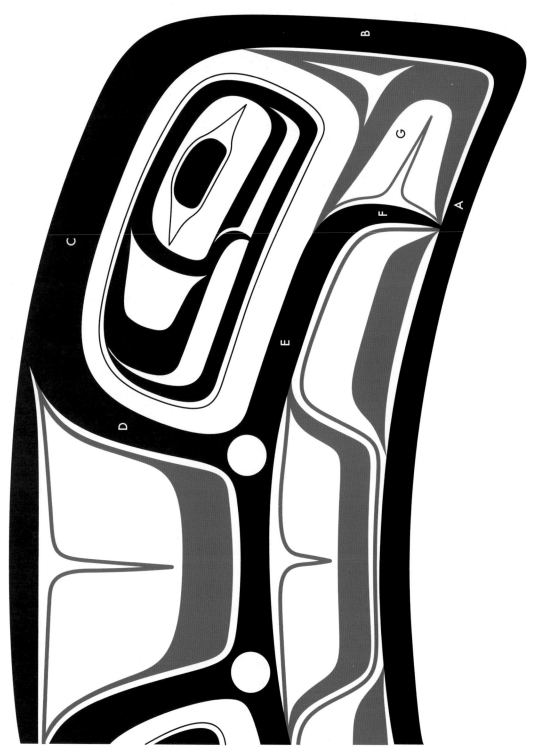

36 Detail of typical face design from a painted box. Private collection.

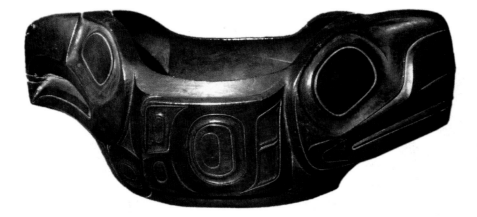

37 Carved wooden grease dish, Haida. The formline plan of the relief carving on the bowl is continued in the organization of the sculptural heads. The cheek design on the whale's head (*right*) could be described as a tertiary solid U enclosed by a secondary formline U with attached triangular filler, relieved by a negative T. The divided tertiary S at the base of the whale's flipper is somewhat uncommon. Royal British Columbia Museum 410.

remaining space. Another painting on a small Haida coffin, in black only, shows the eye socket outline clearly, although the space usually occupied by the cheek is left undecorated (Fig. 40).

These cheek designs range from very simple single secondary elements to elaborate secondary-tertiary complexes. All, however, are variations on two basic patterns. The simplest (which I will designate Type 1) is a secondary L-shaped form which nearly fills the space bounded by eye socket ovoid, jaw formline, and corner of the mouth. The two lower corners are rounded, while the two upper corners are pointed and fair into the primary formlines (Fig. 41). Type 2, perhaps more frequently encountered than the other, consists of a secondary U extension of the side of the mouth and an attached triangular filler (Fig. 42). The examples illustrated do not begin to exhaust the supply of variations.

A curious angularity of the corners and ends of the eye socket ovoid is often seen in face designs of the long "double-eye" type. In at least one specimen (NMC VII C107) it is repeated in the "double-eyes" themselves.

Hands, Feet, and Claws

The joints of human hands and the feet of mammals and birds are rendered typically by an ovoid joint symbol which is proportioned according to the space requirements and, to some extent, the creature represented (Figs. 44 and 45). To this ovoid are attached the required fingers or claws. Hands are shown palm forward, with the fingers extended and slightly separated. The outer edges of the little finger and thumb are tangent to the sides of the base ovoid, and a considerable space is left between thumb and index finger. Usually the spaces

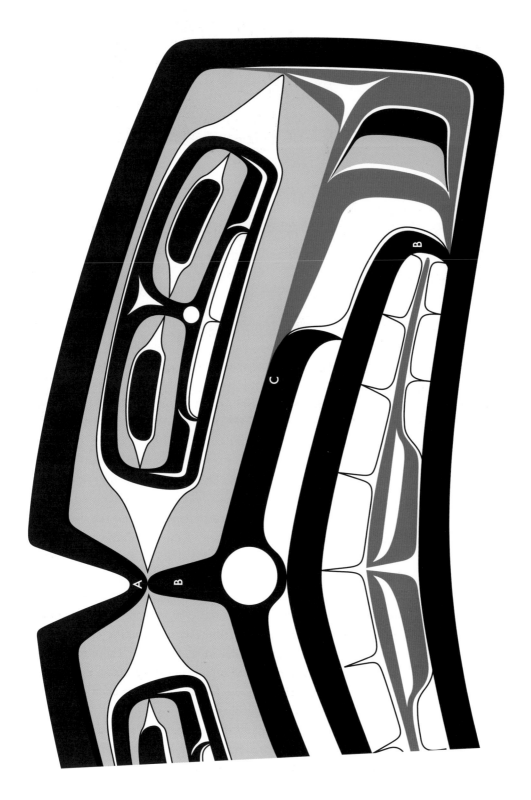

38 Detail of the long eye socket or "double-eye" form of face design.

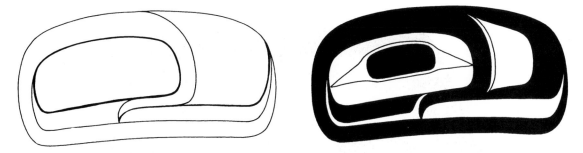

39 Construction of a typical "salmon-trout's-head" inner ovoid.

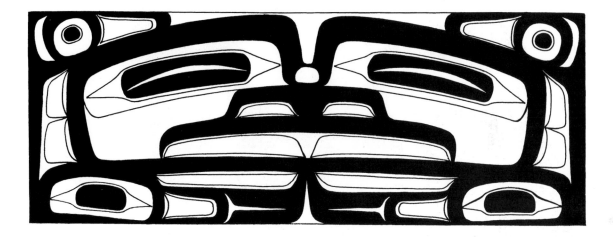

40 Painted design on a coffin, Haida.

between the fingers extend to the inner edge of the formline ovoid of the joint design. Animal and bird feet are shown typically with two large claws, with or without an opposed thumblike claw, or with three large claws without the thumb. The ovoid joint design is not always present. The tips of the claws are bent sharply down and are sometimes relieved at the bend by thin crescent-shaped "slits," or by notches on the inside of the bend.

In configurative designs, where the space-filling requirements are less rigid, the form of foot and claw was perhaps determined largely by the conventions of representing specific creatures. In designs of more abstract arrangement, especially those of the distributive type, the problems of organizing every square inch of surface were so great that the exact form must have been influenced largely by the shape of available space.

Hands, feet, legs, and arms are given the secondary color in about half of the cases in which they occur in painted designs (arms and legs 60/113, hands and feet 65/123).

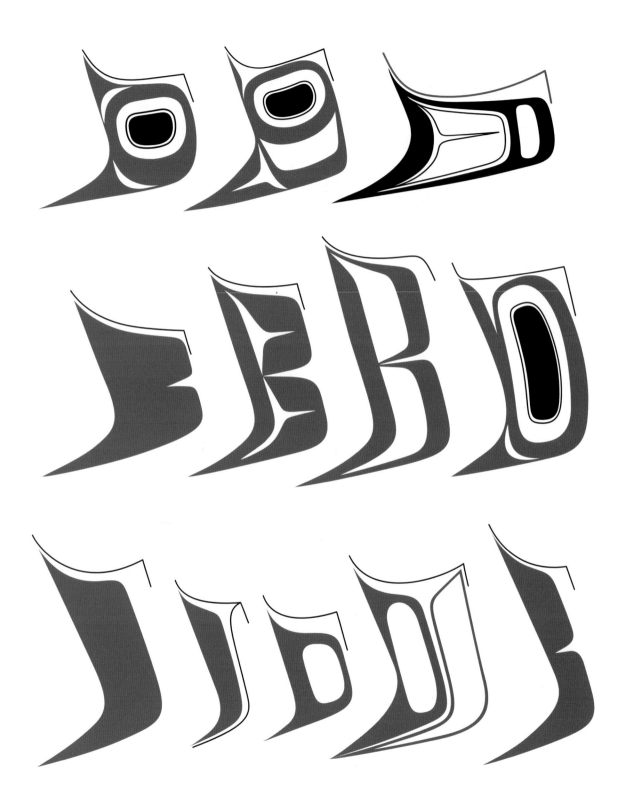

41 Cheek design variations, Type 1.

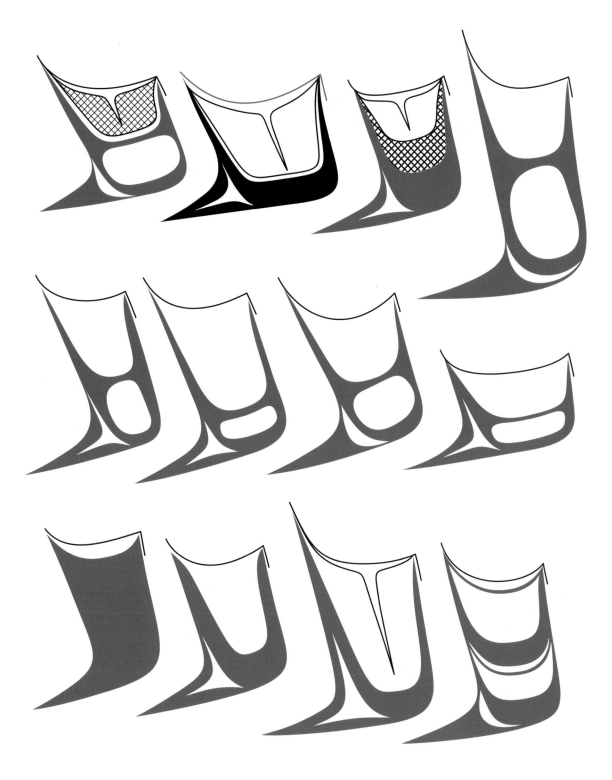

Cheek design variations, Type 2.

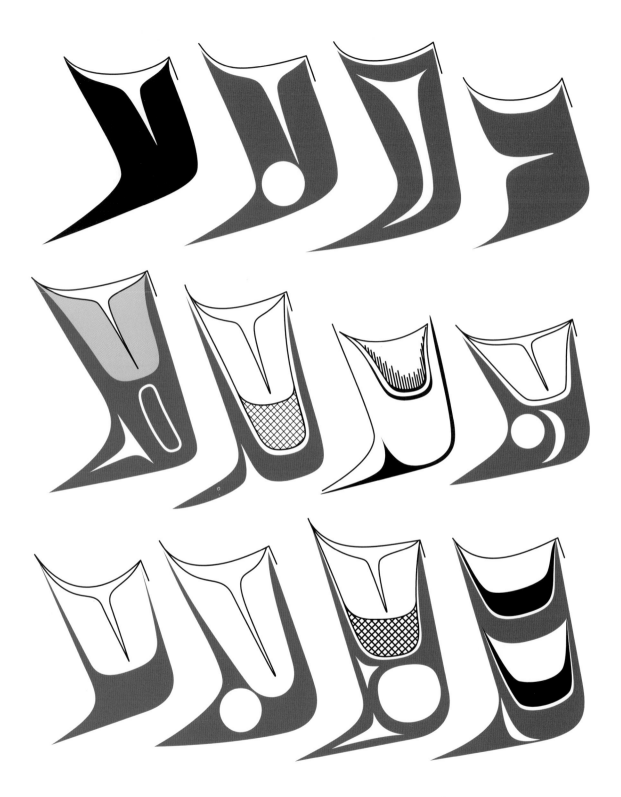

42B Cheek design variations, Type 2.

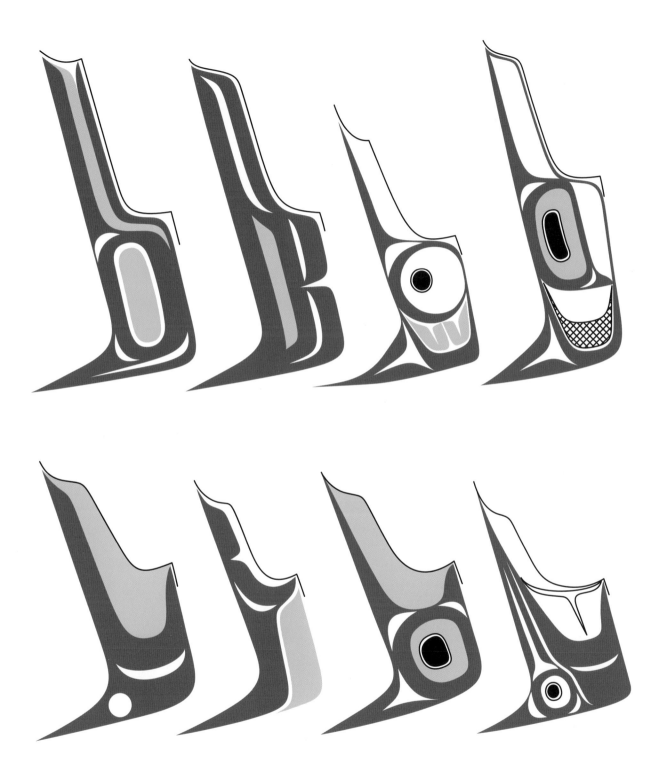

43 Cheek design variations, long "double-eye" type.

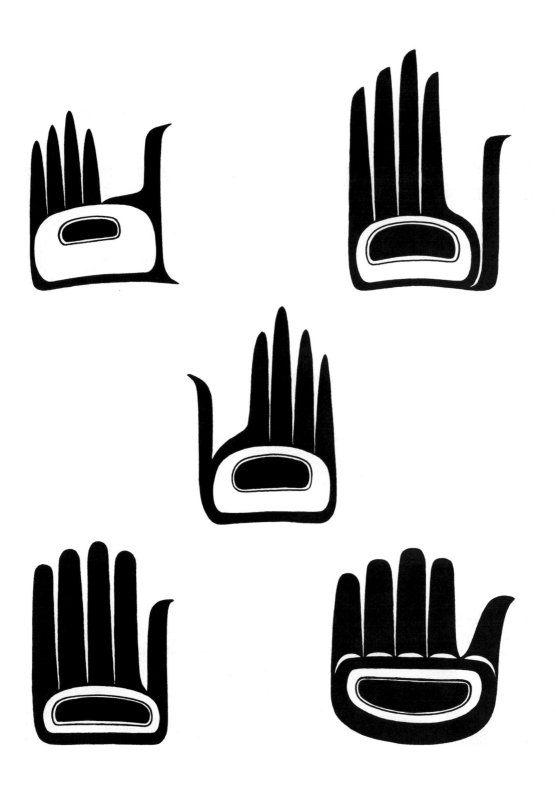

44 Human hands.

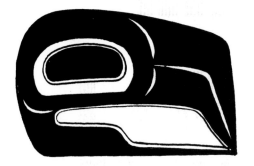

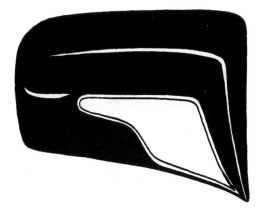

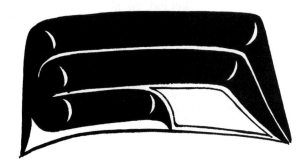

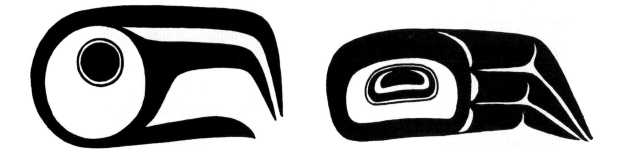

45 Feet of various mammals and birds.

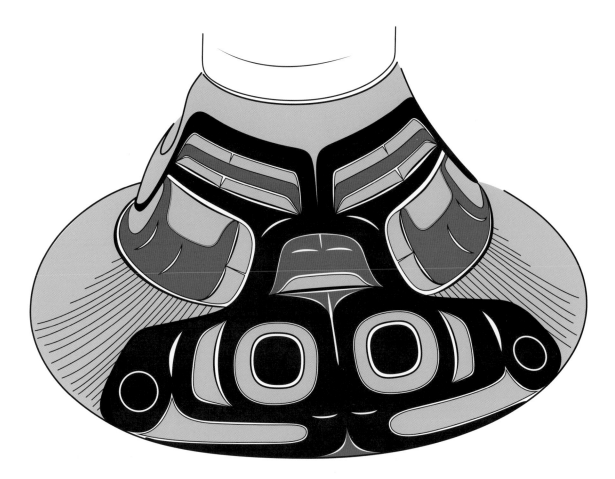

46 Detail of a wooden helmet, Tlingit. The body, flippers, and tail of a whale are represented in this carved and painted formline design on the well-known Killer Whale Hat of Chief Shakes. Burke Museum catalogue number 1-1436.

Resultant Forms

Whenever two or more positive forms approach each other in a design, there is a space that can be considered negative between them. This space has a shape that results from the combined shapes of the adjacent edges of the positive forms, and it may therefore be termed a *resultant form*. The skilled Indian artist was able to control the shapes and relative positions of the positive forms so as to control the resultant forms. Probably all tertiary units are basically resultant forms which have become more or less standardized owing to the frequent use of certain combinations of primary and secondary (positive) forms. That tertiary units may be considered as related to negative area, or ground, is demonstrated by the fact that many objects, such as wooden hats, are commonly painted blue-green over their plain surface, with any two-dimensional design apparently superimposed on this ground color, the same color used in tertiary units (Fig. 46).

Transitional Devices

The simplest of all the methods used to join one form to another was to place one form tangent to another. A second method was to overlap, in effect, the joining formlines. Both of these methods result in heavy, unrelieved color areas at the point of joining and apparently offended the sensitivities of the artists, because they were seldom used without modification (Fig. 47). This usually consisted of narrowing one or both formlines at the juncture so that the total width was not increased materially.

The very close relationship in form between one unit and another is demonstrated in the joining of ovoids and U's. Very frequently the outer edge of a formline ovoid forms the inner edge of the adjacent (overlapped) formline U. Usually the ovoid is less distorted by the inevitable modification at the initial point of overlap of the two forms (Fig. 47A).

Specific Transitional Devices

When one formline joins another, the junction is relieved in one of several ways (Fig. 48). In *straight juncture*, the joining formline diminishes and joins a formline unit at a corner, continuing the direction of the joined formline (Fig. 48A). In *square juncture*, the joining formline diminishes to a point and joins another formline at nearly a right angle (Fig. 48B). In *turning juncture*, the joining

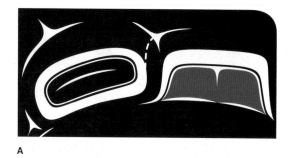

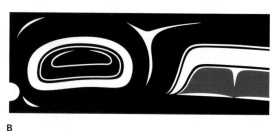

A

B

formline diminishes and turns to fair into the joined formline (Fig. 48C). In *swelling juncture*, the joining formline swells and joins, with the heavy juncture relieved by a T-shaped or crescent-shaped negative "slit" that defines the edges of the joined formlines, or with a negative circle that suggests the limits of the formlines. This circle cuts far into them, often nearly to their outer edges (Fig. 48D). The effect of the use of these transitional devices is to define forms at their juncture with other forms, to eliminate unduly heavy color areas, and to maintain the easy flow of form throughout the whole design.

Nine examples of solid, right-angle junctures without transitional devices were recorded. Since they were first noticed after the recording of characteristics had been under way for some time, it is possible that their incidence might be greater than the tabulation shows. All recorded examples are from square boxes with two opposite, symmetrically organized, painted sides, and the unrelieved junctures are in every case at one end or both ends of the vertical formlines delineating the sides of the animal's body (Fig. 49).

Relief of Inner Ovoids

The "iris" or inner ovoid unit in eye and joint designs is sometimes solid black and sometimes relieved. The usual method of relieving this black area was to treat it as a formline ovoid with the negative central area nonconcentric so that the upper formline of the ovoid was very thin. Within this space was placed another positive ovoid, its upper edge tangent to the upper edge of the enclosing form (Fig. 50). The resultant negative space is a C-shaped form (Fig. 51A). Occasionally in paintings and commonly in Chilkat weaving, the inner ovoid is completely surrounded by the negative space (Fig. 51B).

47 Two examples from the same box design (Canadian Museum of History catalogue number VII B 139), illustrating methods of joining adjacent ovoids and U's. A is the usual method of overlapping, in effect, the primary formlines so as not to increase their width, and defining one of the joined units with a relieving "slit." This technique of joining formlines is made possible by the close formal relationship of units so that the outer edge of the ovoid conforms to the inner edge of the U. B illustrates another method in which the units are placed side by side, essentially unaltered by the relieving slit that separates them.

48 Detail of the design from a painted box. Private collection.

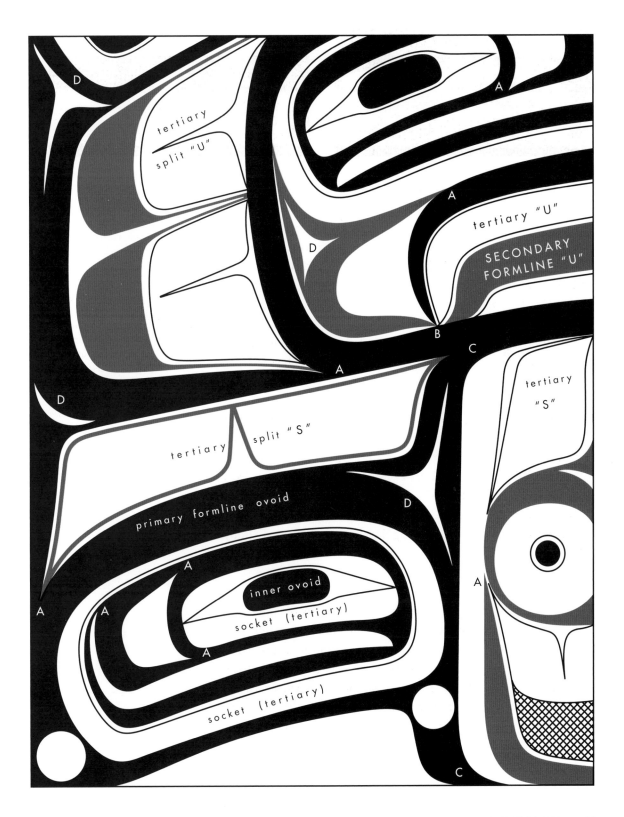

tertiary
split "U"

D

A

A

tertiary "U"

SECONDARY
FORMLINE "U"

D

B

C

tertiary
"S"

D

tertiary   split "S"

primary formline ovoid

D

A

A

inner ovoid

socket (tertiary)

A

A

A

A

socket (tertiary)

C

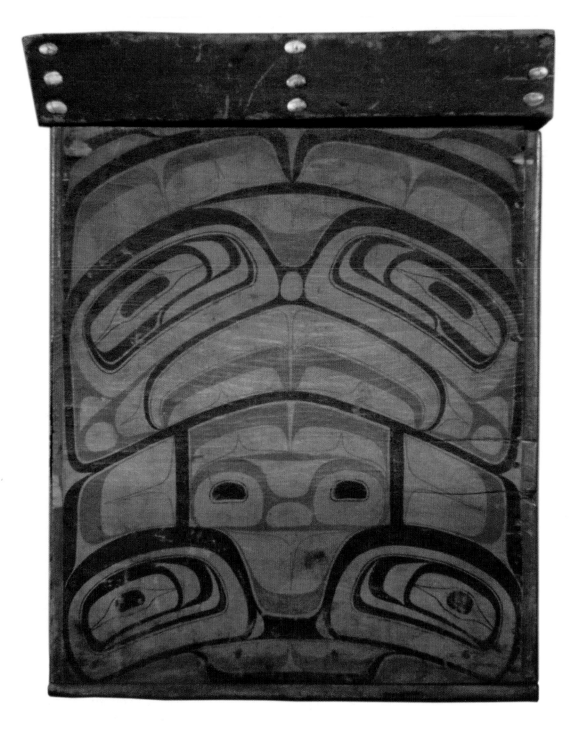

49 Painted square box. Unrelieved solid right-angle junctures appear at each corner of the central design field. Museum of Northern British Columbia.

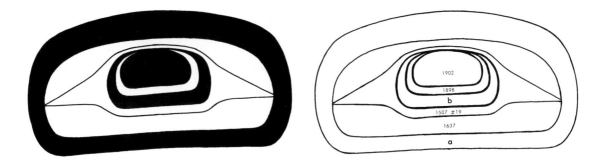

Labels within image b:
1902
1898
b
1507 #19
1637
a

50 Development of an eye design with templates from the Washington State Museum. Templates *a* and *b* by the author.

A third variant is the introduction of a horizontal slit with tapering, slightly downward-curved ends across the center of the inner ovoid. This is most frequently seen in Chilkat weaving, but it also occurs in carved and painted designs (Fig. 51C).

Formlines themselves are sometimes lightened by negative design areas. One method is to introduce a long eyelid with enclosed iris into the formline (Fig. 51D).

Line

True line is used frequently in Northwest Coast art. There is always such a line drawn around an iris design that is not enclosed by an eyelid line. A similar line parallels the inside edge of many U forms, and makes the long central divider of the split U. No such line typically parallels the inner edge of a formline ovoid. Of the two exceptions (2/400), one was rated 1 and the other 4 on a "quality of workmanship" scale with a range of 1 to 4.

The tertiary function of true line has been mentioned (p. 32). The use of such an outline greatly softens the contrast of the outlined form with its background.

Textures

There are two texturelike patterns that occur frequently in the art, *hatching* and *dashing*. Hatching, either simple or cross-hatching, is used in two ways: (1) It indicates ground and some tertiary forms in unpainted objects such as engraved metal work, slate platters, some soapberry spoons, some carved dishes, and similar objects (73/131) (Fig. 52). (2) In painted objects it can be used on certain secondary and tertiary units, especially U forms and eye sockets of extraneous faces (107/268). It is always red or black, never blue-green.

Hatching creates, in effect, another color (or two others, if both black and red are used [34/97]) in the scheme. However, its greatest

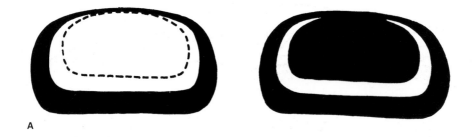

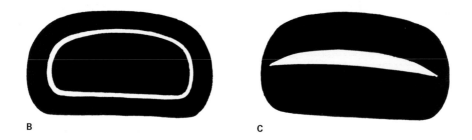

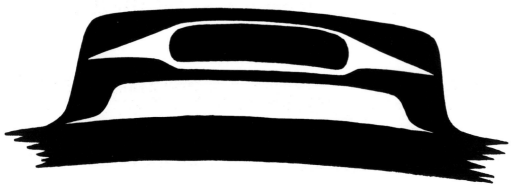

51 Relief of heavy areas of color. (A) Construction of a negative C in an inner ovoid.
(B) Concentric ovoid relief of an inner ovoid. (C) Horizontal slit relief of an inner ovoid.
(D) Eye relief of a formline U.

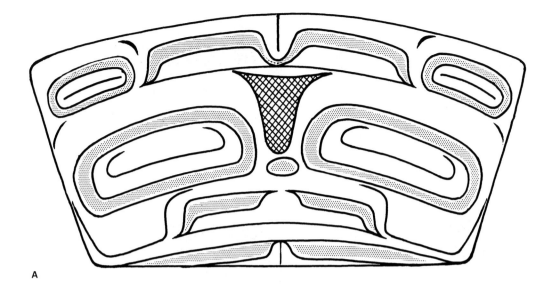

A

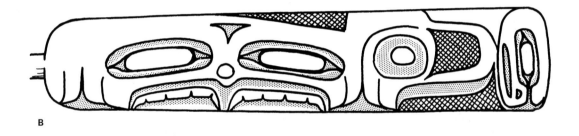

B

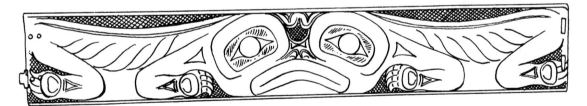

C

52 (A) End of a carved dish, Stikine Tlingit. (B) Carved soapberry spoon, Tlingit.
(C) Engraved silver bracelet. Burke Museum catalogue numbers 1405, 2217, 2342.

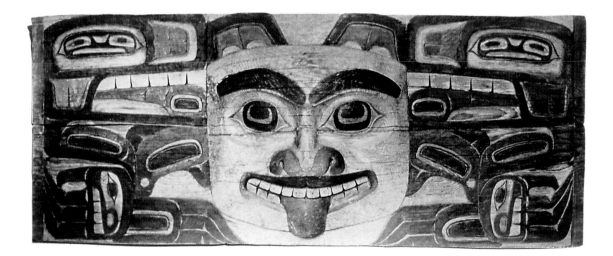

53 Coffin front from a mortuary pole, Haida. The Field Museum 9974.

value lies in the relief it affords from the constantly flowing, curvilinear, nonconcentric aspect of the total design. Hatching, with its angularity, its evenly spaced, constant width lines and unrelieved intersections, is in direct contrast to the general fluidity. The hatched area, however, always assumes a shape that relates it to the larger design.

A variant of hatching is dashing, consisting of parallel lines, usually broken at intervals to form groups of aligned parallel dashes in series. These, either in black or in red, are used principally in eye sockets of extraneous faces and other tertiary units (Figs. 35A and 54).

Occasionally red dashing is superimposed on blue or black areas. This use adds a new effect of transparency, another relief to the almost constant opacity of the painting. When so used on blue it gives a definite purple cast to the affected area. When the red is vermilion and the blue is the cobalt hue favored by the Bella Bella and

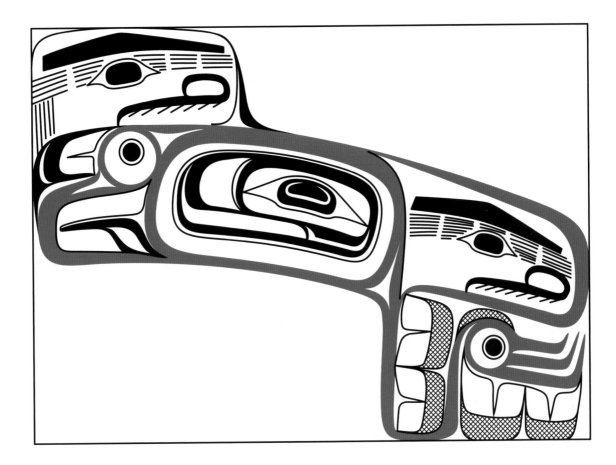

54 Painted design on the end of a carved and painted chest, Haida. Burke Museum catalogue number 2291.

Bella Coola, the effect is one of great richness and intensity (Von Sydow, 1932:Pl. XVII).

Absence of Overlapping

A device frequently found in representational art is the use of overlapping to achieve the effect of depth in a flat design. It is not surprising that the highly formalized and decorative northern two-dimensional art seldom produced examples of this. Only a few cases of overlapping have been seen, although it occurs frequently in the sculpture of the region. The very well-known painting of the sea wolf in Boas' *Primitive Art*, Fig. 134, exhibits overlapping in the two whales held in the ears and tail of the monster. A much more surprising example, in that body parts which ordinarily would be handled in a perfectly flat manner are strongly overlapped, is a Haida coffin front in the Chicago Natural History Museum (Fig. 53). Here everything works according to rule except that the hind feet of the bear overlap the front feet by one third in such a way that there can be no doubt that an overlap was intended from the start. There is ample room for the front paws to have been shown in their entirety with only a slight modification, well within conventional limits, of their proportions.

Principles of Form and Organization

Total Use of the Given Space

In Northwest Coast art, as in any art, "the given surface is the primary condition of composition and its utilization as an esthetic factor presents to the artist ever new problems" (Haeberlin, 1918:261). This does not imply that the given surface must be filled entirely with the design for a successful solution to the compositional problem. It means that the artist must be aware of the total space and the effect on that space of any element he introduces to it. If we consider the "total use of the given space" to be a principle of two-dimensional design of the Northwest Coast, it follows that, especially with designs of the configurative type, the artist must not merely place a design, fine as it may be, in the middle of any given space, but must use all of his sensitivity to relate that design to the total space and to control the shape of the ground or negative space. Examination of examples of Northwest Coast art will show this to be the rule (Fig. 54).

Adjustment of Form to Surface

Haeberlin (1918:261) says that "the most striking demonstration of the esthetic sense of the northwest coast artist lies in the adaptation of his subject matter to a given surface." Here, perhaps, he refers specifically to the fitting of the design exactly to the space, which, of course, is one of the great triumphs of the Northwest Coast artists and is most emphatically demonstrated in the magnificently carved and painted boxes and chests (Fig. 55).

Total Organization of Space

The northern artist's approach to his problem no longer can be documented, except as it survives in a much modified form. Garfield's description of the making of a box design by a Nisqa artist in 1934 (Garfield, 1955b:165–68 and Pl. IV) is the most complete description of the process to be seen. Although the finished box design is not at all like those on most of the fine boxes we have seen in refinement and detail, its organization is similar to that described here, and the artist very probably approached the problem in a rather traditional way. Using templates cut from cardboard, he laid out the design directly on the final surface, a sheet of drawing paper representing the side of the box. No preliminary sketches or layouts were made, and few false starts or changes in developing the design were recorded. At one point, he, "with his pencil in midair, traced

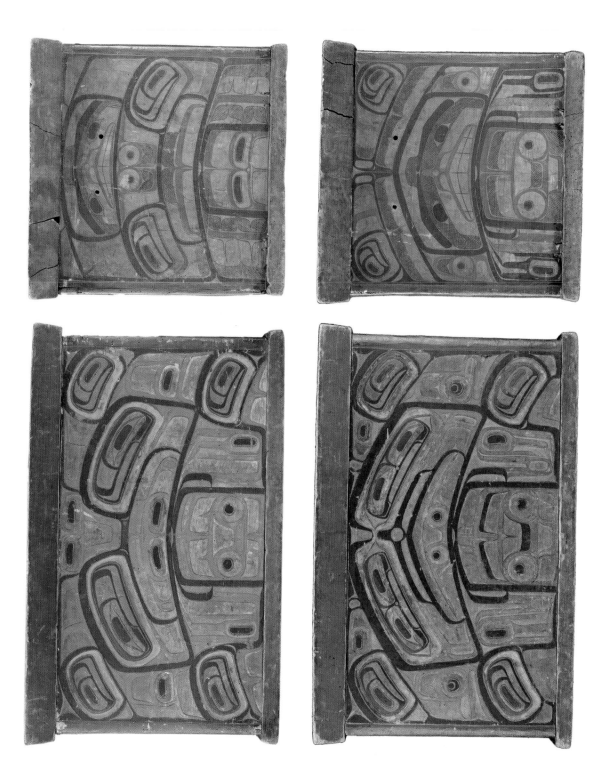

imaginary lines" (Garfield, 1955b:167). Present-day Kwakiutl artists work in much the same way, directly on the finished surface, with no sketching or visible planning, whether they are products of the old-time apprentice system or young men responding to the renewed interest in tribal art.

It seems impossible that the elaborate and superlatively refined designs on old chests, for example, could have been planned without benefit of preliminary sketches. Boas' statement (referring to North American Indians generally), "Perhaps the artists have greater eidetic power than most adults among ourselves" (Boas, 1927:158), may be well founded.

The task of isolating and describing the characteristics of form in Northwest Coast art is a simple one compared to the problem of analyzing its organization, for here the Indian artist demonstrated his great sensitivity and mastery of the idiom. The very fact that "art" is involved makes objective analysis difficult. It would be handy if a Northwest Coast "Golden Mean" could be discovered to apply to the proportion and arrangement of elements within a design. We can be reasonably sure, however, that the native artist used no such system of ratios and proportions in his approach to composition, even though the results of his efforts invite one to analyze them in geometric terms.

Boas surely did not mean to imply Indian use, for compositional purposes, of lines drawn from the corners to the centers of the long sides of the decorated faces of chests (Boas, 1927:266). He qualifies his remarks concerning the passage of these lines through certain points in the design with "almost always," "often," and "generally." My own experiments with them lead me to say that they "sometimes" pass through the specified points.

Most of the large chests examined do show designs falling in one of several more or less set compositions, and other types of boxes and dishes are commonly decorated with respectively characteristic arrangements of design, which Boas describes (Boas, 1927: 265–77). These compositions were all somewhat flexible, and within their framework infinite variation and elaboration was possible (Fig. 56).

Compositional Factors

The arrangement of a composition was influenced by a number of factors, not the least of which was the *creature represented*. This was particularly true in designs of the configurative type, and it certainly

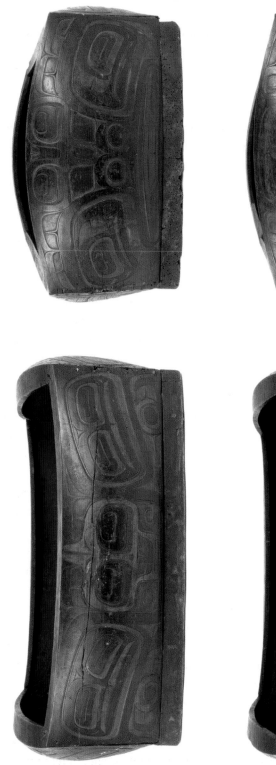

PRINCIPLES OF FORM AND ORGANIZATION

56 Large carved bent-corner dish, Skide-gate Haida. Canadian Museum of History, catalogue number VII B 739, image numbers S86-1418–S86-1421.

applied, to a lesser degree, to expansive and distributive designs. In the case of configurative design, the general outline of the design and the proportions and relative positions of the body parts were, subject to conventionalized distortion and emphasis, determined by the type of creature to be shown and the space within which the design was to be disposed.

When the degree of realism was less and the overall decorative aspect prevailed, the influence of representation on the composition declined and the *given space* became the more important compositional factor (Fig. 57). Representation had its influence on even the most highly abstracted distributive design, however, so that when the conventions of the art become familiar one can recognize, for example, the large double-profile heads and constricted bodies on the faces of carved and painted chests and painted square boxes.

The *form of design elements* was another factor affecting design arrangement. It has been shown that individual elements had somewhat fixed forms, which could be modified in shape and proportion within limits. These elements were attached to one another in prescribed ways and in certain spatial relationships. The conventions extended even to the form of the resultant negative spaces or grounds. The Indian artist was so skilled that no square inch of even the most elaborate distributive design was left to chance, but every form, positive and negative, fitted without strain into the whole pattern, and every element conformed in all its parts and relationships to the system described here.

The compositional factor that depended to the greatest degree upon the sensitivity of the individual artist, assuming his understanding of symbolism, the form of elements, and their spatial relationships, was the *distribution of weight and balance*. The usually black formline pattern establishing the main forms of the design was given a remarkably even distribution. Within the spaces thus formed were placed tertiary elements and smaller patterns in the secondary color. These often were secondary complexes and were constructed of formlines similar to the primary formlines or slightly smaller in scale, and more compactly arranged. The distribution of these secondary complexes was such that the degree of detail was fairly uniform throughout the whole design (Fig. 21). They were sometimes further elaborated with "subsecondary" elements of their own in the contrasting, or primary, color. These subsecondary elements were almost always isolated, that is, they rarely formed

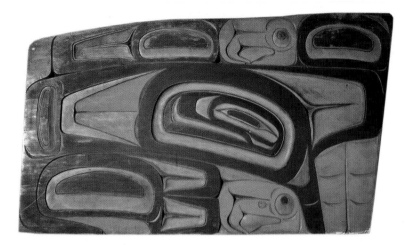

57 Carved and painted settee, Haida. (A) Inner face of side panel. (B) Back panel with drawing of attached side panels and seat. The Field Museum 79595.

A

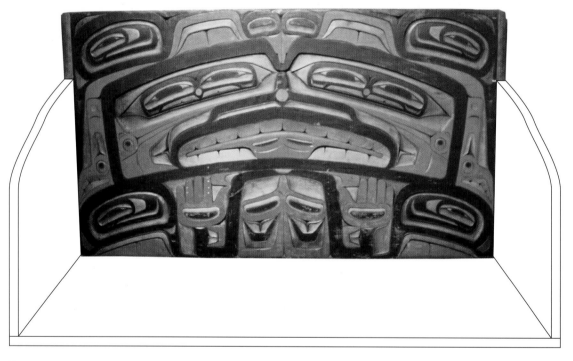

B

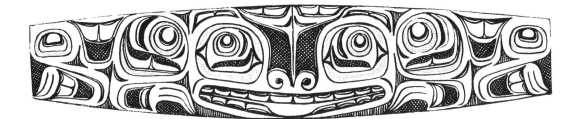

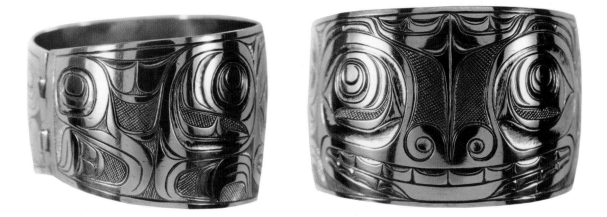

58 Engraved silver bracelet, Haida. University of British Columbia Museum of Anthropology 8094. Photograph by Nancy Harris.

complexes, and, when they did, these were of the simplest type, usually a pair of U forms. As stated before, the inner ovoid in eye and joint designs was almost invariably painted black, but it belongs in the same class, primary or secondary, with the complex of which it is a part. Its thin line border is actually a part of the tertiary area that surrounds it.

Relative Simplicity

In spite of great apparent detail and complexity, elaboration was carried only to a rather fixed degree, which tended to keep the design open. First, a large, open, and continuous primary formline design delineates the main body parts. Second, a similarly large, compact arrangement of secondary units fills the outstanding spaces remaining, except those, such as sockets, which are entirely tertiary. Third, this large primary-secondary design of even weight and distribution is elaborated with isolated subsecondary and tertiary elements, directly related to and similar in form to the large elements.

No further elaboration takes place, whether the design is spread over the front of a house or wrapped around a silver bracelet (Fig. 58). The scale of design detail is totally unrelated to the size of the

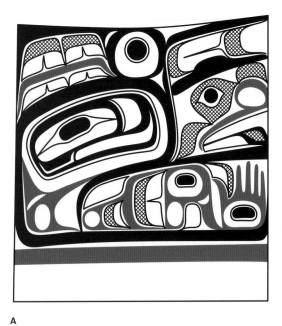

A

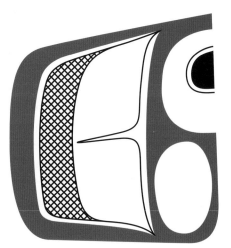

B

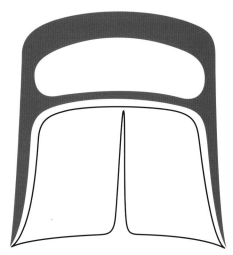

C

D

59 Relation of total organization to individual design units. (A) Painted box. (B) Design unit from A. The shape and proportion of the large pattern are mirrored in this component unit. (C) Painted box. (D) Design unit from C. Burke Museum Walker Loan numbers 1507-108, 1507-106.

decorated object, but is a function of the system of primary, secondary, tertiary, and subsecondary construction. Perhaps such relative simplicity is a factor in the "monumentality" of many small Northwest Coast pieces that has intrigued observers (Inverarity, 1950: Fig. 49; Boas, 1927; Gunther, 1962:8).

Relation to Unit Form

The entire composition conforms to the rules governing the shape and proportion of its individual design units, especially in designs of the distributive type, as on the sides of chests and boxes. Symmetrical designs, for example, seem to be organized similarly to ovoids or U units (Fig. 59B). The main formlines at the top take a convex curve, and those at the bottom suggest a curve that varies according to the proportions of the box side, even as the corresponding curve of an ovoid varies according to its own proportions. Box designs that are not symmetrical can often be likened to U or S units if they do not fall in the ovoid category (Fig. 59A). A detailed discussion of the organization of a number of box designs has been given by Boas (1927:262–78) in which he notes the great curvature of the designs at the top, diminishing toward the bottom, which is ascribed to a "tendency to avoid massing of parallel lines." The same tendency applies to the construction of individual design units. Boas also discusses in some detail the symbolism of the designs as well as the arrangement of design units.

Full-Face Square Boxes

Tall boxes with a square plan, painted on two opposite faces with symmetrical "full-face" designs, are not described by Boas, although they are frequently seen in collections (Fig. 60). They all fall into a general pattern of organization, with a large head (including ears or other upper ornaments) covering nearly the upper half of the design from one edge to the other. This head is more or less strongly curved up in the center, with the upper curve more pronounced, as usual. Very often the face on one side shows the simple "salmon-trout's-head" development of the eye with deep (and often wide) interorbital separation and no apparent nostrils, while the opposite face takes an elaborated form with long nostrils, shallow angular forehead notch, and "double-eye." Below the large head there is a smaller, roughly rectangular body area flanked by two narrower fields in which the front legs, flippers, or wings of the represented creature are displayed. The symbolism is often very obscure. The lower field is the narrowest of the three and commonly contains two large joint designs. The distribution of parts is very similar to that of the large chests except that the joint designs at the bottom are placed under the body rather than flanking it (Fig. 61). This primary arrangement results in from nine to fifteen secondary complexes, with most of the variation coming in the extreme upper and lower fields.

The paintings on the remaining two sides of these painted boxes are unique and deserve further study (Fig. 62). Generally they appear incomplete or fragmentary—merely template-drawn outlines of floating ovoids or rudimentary complexes. Sometimes they are quite unlike anything else in Northwest Coast painting (Fig. 60). Some of them seem to be related to the geometric designs painted on the tops of spruce root hats (Figs. 7 and 62B). These designs, like those on the ends of many large carved chests, are almost never exactly alike on the two sides, and they appear to be unrelated symbolically and compositionally to the main decorated areas. Their independence is emphasized by the fact that the direction of movement of the design is repeated, rather than reversed to correspond to the symmetrical arrangement of the main design (Fig. 61). The simplicity of these end paintings imparts a feeling of restraint and elegance to the otherwise richly decorated surface.

Certain other classes of decorated objects, for example, soul catchers, raven rattles, coppers, and the like, also seem to have had somewhat standardized surface design organization, although there was apparently much less systematization in the design of these objects than in chests and boxes (Fig. 63). Many two-dimensionally decorated objects were entirely products of the artist's imagination and skill at handling the conventions of the art. His effort was always directed toward relating the decoration to the surface, representing the given creature, and achieving even distribution of weight and detail within the flowing and continuous primary formline structure with its secondary and tertiary elaborations. The organization of his design was influenced strongly by the conventional form of elements and by traditional emphasis on the head and certain key features of the subject animal.

Positive-Negative Space

The spaces between positive shapes must be considered part of the design and were carefully controlled. This is most easily seen in a

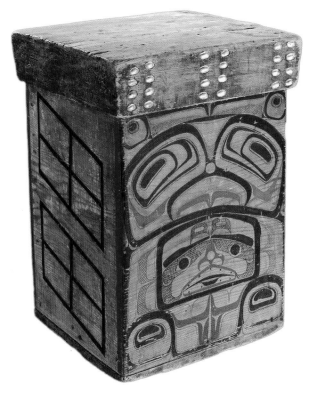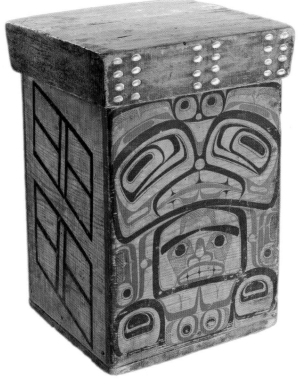

60 The four sides of a square box, Massett Haida. Most boxes of this type show the double-eye development of the face on one side. Image cpn09937 courtesy of Royal B.C. Museum, B.C. Archives.

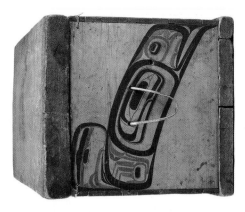

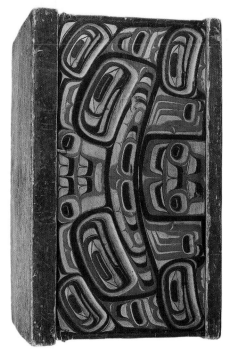

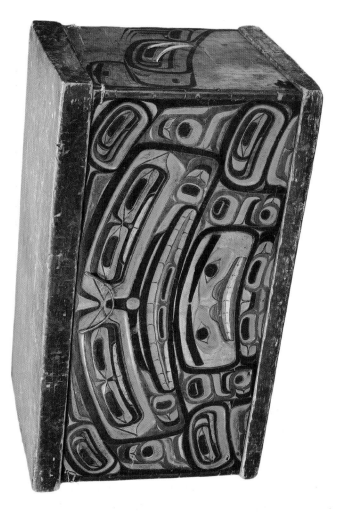

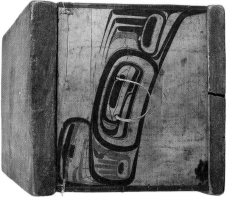

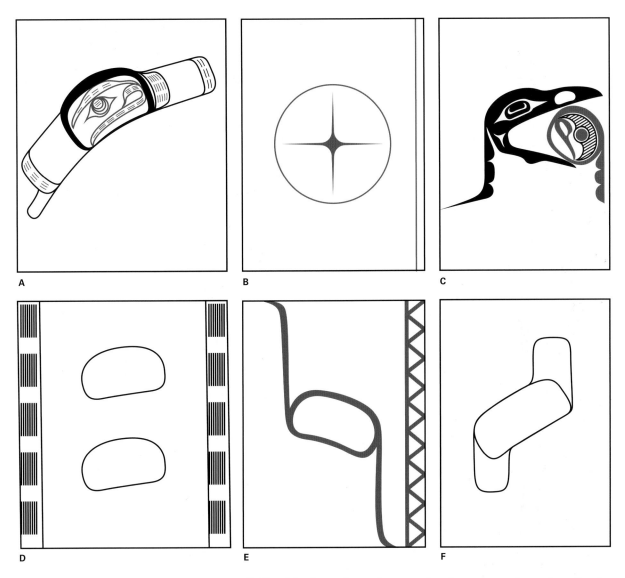

A

B

C

D

E

F

62 Designs from the sides of square boxes. Burke Museum Walker Loan number 1507-62, Burke Museum catalogue numbers 1-10803, 6868 (*left to right, top*); private collection, Royal British Columbia Museum 9743, private collection (*left to right, bottom*).

Chilkat blanket, where the negative shapes are often taken for the positive primary design by those not familiar with the fact that the primary design is black. When the blanket (where the negative and tertiary shapes and secondary designs predominate because of their color) is compared with its pattern board (which has a predominantly black design), this relationship is easily seen. The importance of the negative shape is also seen in appliqué work, where seemingly isolated negative shapes actually define the positive shapes (Fig. 64).

No understanding of the organization and form of northern Northwest Coast two-dimensional art can take place without rec-

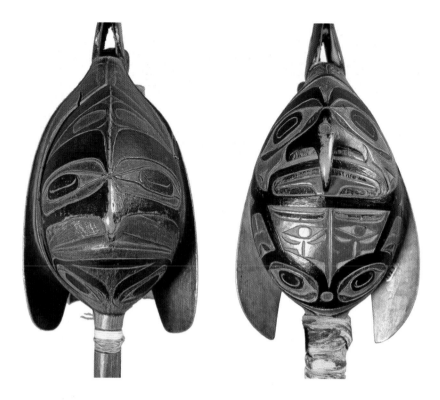

63 Details of two raven rattles. Burke Museum catalogue numbers 2823, 1-31.

ognition of the function of the primary formline and its relation to negative space. I have seen some contemporary Haida silver pieces that illustrate this very well (Fig. 66). The maker of a brace-let of fine workmanship, apparently copied from an illustration of an older specimen (B.C. Indian Arts and Welfare Society, 1948), had visualized the creature as a solid figure upon which various small design units were disposed. He did not recognize the existence of the primary formline pattern in the original, with its resultant negative shapes. Consequently the secondary and tertiary units, whose form and position are determined by these negative shapes, were incorrectly formed and placed. The departure from traditional arrangement is obvious as soon as the primary formline pattern is visualized.

This lack of understanding of the important function of the pri-mary formline is seen in many published illustrations of Northwest Coast art. The color plates in Emmons' *The Whale House of the Chilkat* (Emmons, 1916), although drawn from photographs, are examples. A comparison between these illustrations and photographs of the "Rain Wall" and the house posts, with their two-dimensional surface decoration, plainly shows that the illustrator either disre-

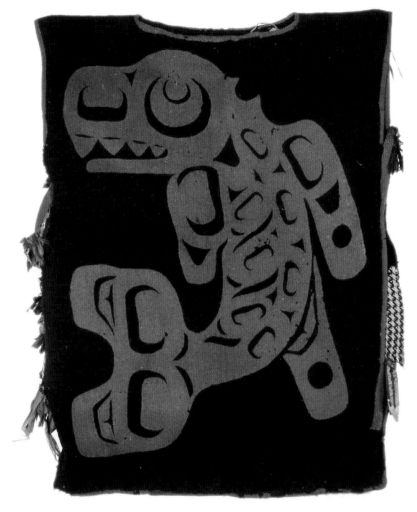

64 Woolen appliqué shirt, Haida. Burke Museum catalogue number 2.

garded, or failed to recognize, the formline patterns and the actual form of the primary, secondary, and tertiary elements. These masterpieces clearly exhibit all the characteristics of organization and form described in this study, including continuity of primary and secondary formline patterns, semiangularity of curves, relative simplicity, and so forth (Fig. 67). Little of this is apparent in Emmons' color plates.

The formline pattern is easily seen in designs in which the formlines are thin in relation to the formed spaces, especially if these are painted (Fig. 68). The formline structure in some specimens is so massive that transitional devices and ground are reduced to thin lines and slits (Fig. 69). Since these slits define the limits of formline units, their positions and forms are very critical. The difficulty in

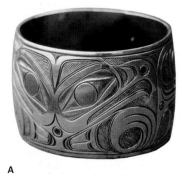

A

65 (A) Silver bracelet by Charles Edensaw, Haida. (B) Detail. Catalogue number
13064, Royal British Columbia Museum.
Photograph by Nancy Harris.

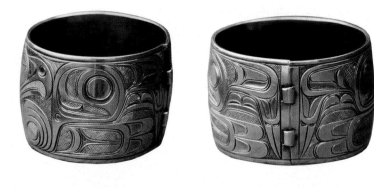

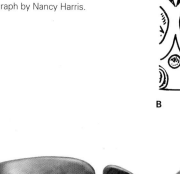

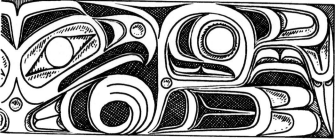

B

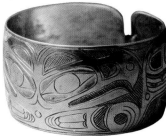

A

66 (A) Silver bracelet recently made in
the Queen Charlotte Islands, Haida. This
bracelet was copied from a drawing of
the Edensaw bracelet published in *Native
Designs of British Columbia*. It is somewhat unfair to compare it with the work
of one of the great masters of Haida art,
but the comparison illustrates graphically
the fundamental position of formline
structure in the art. (B) Detail. Private
collection. Photograph by Nancy Harris.

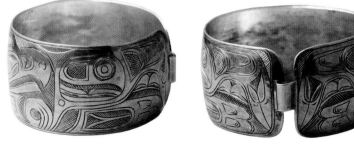

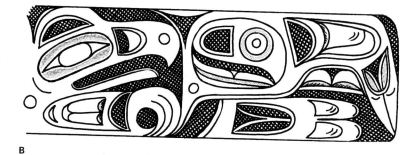

B

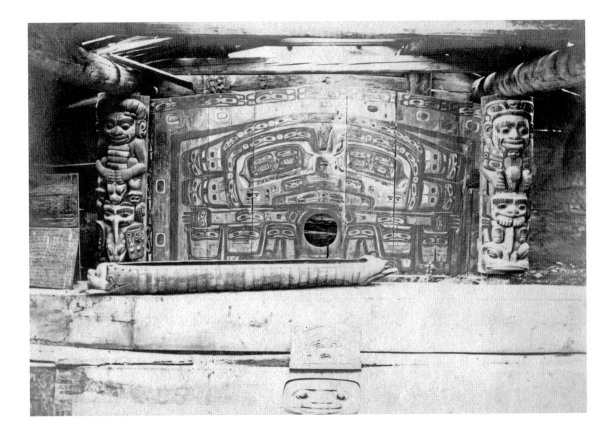

67 Interior of the Whale House, Klukwan. University of Washington Libraries, Special Collections, NA 3071.

seeing the formline pattern is increased if the design is carved but not painted, since the difference between primary and secondary areas is not apparent.

Movement

The fact that this is primarily a curvilinear art emphasizes the effect of movement, in the artistic sense. All design has movement; the problem for the artist is that of "organizing the perception movements so that they will create a closed and self-sufficient circuit" (Scott, 1951:37). Movement in Northwest Coast art certainly fulfills these requirements. A sensitive arrangement of related forms is bound together with a network of subtly varied line, meandering purposefully over the surface, merging, dividing, and curving to every corner of the design. If it were not for the relief of hatched areas and near angularity in the corners of forms, the fluidity of this art could be burdensome, but the sensitive artist recognized and controlled the flow. The movement of the design is entirely self-contained. It may carry to the very edge of the decorated area, but always returns at the last instant, never tempting the viewer to leave the little universe of the design.

Use of the Formline

The use of the swelling and constricting formline delineating design units is one of the most important characteristics of the art and should be considered a principle of it.

Semiangularity of Curves

The sudden changes from gentle curve to sharp curve and back to gentle curve are a manifestation of a principle that gives great strength and solidity to this art. The corners of the curvilinear forms are points of tension. They give the flow of the design a pulse or rhythmic emphasis which eliminates the softness common to many curvilinear designs. Junctures with other forms are usually made near these corners.

The degree of angularity of curves varies greatly. A number of specimens have been noted in which the corners of many of the U forms were true angles (Fig. 70). In this respect they resemble the designs in Chilkat weaving. A further similarity lies in the frequent occurrence of small circles set in the centers of secondary and tertiary solid U's, which seem to be commonly associated with the angular form. In some examples the most angular U forms appear together with the most smoothly curved ovoids (Fig. 71).

Symmetry

To a large degree Northwest Coast two-dimensional art is horizontally symmetrical. The principles of splitting and of representing the whole animal naturally lead to bilateral symmetry. Often what appears to be an asymmetric arrangement of design on the side of a box proves to be a reversal of the adjacent side, forming a bilaterally symmetrical design with the axis of symmetry at the corner of the box (Fig. 15). There are, to be sure, many examples of asymmetric design, particularly those of the configurative type. In such cases, however, the principle of bilateral symmetry holds for many of the individual design units. Ovoids and U units are essentially symmetrical within themselves.

Boas (1927:33–34) and others have pointed out the universal predominance of horizontally symmetrical design over vertical symmetry and have suggested physiological reasons. In North-

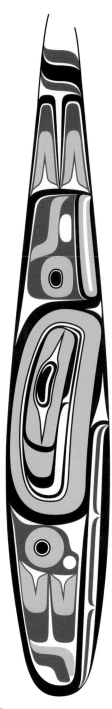

68 Carved and painted canoe paddle. Private collection.

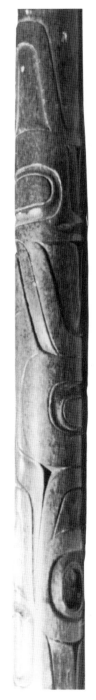

69 Section of a chief's staff, Haida. Courtesy University of British Columbia Museum of Anthropology, Vancouver, Canada, A7086.

west Coast art the use of templates goes hand in hand with the stress on symmetry, both in individual design units and in total organization.

Examples of biaxial symmetry, so very common in the geometric art of the Plains Indians and others, are almost totally lacking. If they are taken as a single design, the decorations on both ends of the long, flat northern feast dishes can be considered biaxially symmetrical. Even here, what appears to be symmetry may be only in the principal organization of the design and not in the detail (Fig. 72). Some carved bowls of mountain sheep horn and wood having a continuous design on the outer surface with an axis of symmetry at each end and in the center of each side could be considered examples of biaxial symmetry (Fig. 73). Still, the intent seems more likely to be two similar designs oriented in opposite directions, since from any normal viewpoint (excluding that from the bottom) only one half of the decorated area can be seen.

The coronalike rim of a beautiful Bella Coola mask (Utzinger, 1922:Pl. 33) is essentially biaxially symmetrical, while another very similar piece (possibly from the same hand, although identified as Haida) in the National Museum of Canada (Royal Ontario Museum, 1959:Fig. A41) suggests this kind of symmetry but has in fact only one axis.

Nonconcentricity

The avoidance of concentricity is closely related to, if not the same as, the avoidance of parallelism. In the typical eye and joint symbols the inner ovoid is above the center, often very much so. This is not always the case in Chilkat weaving, probably owing in part to limitations imposed by the technique. U forms one within the other can also be said to lack concentricity, since the negative space separating the inner and outer forms is often thicker at the end than at the sides. An exception to the rule of nonconcentricity is the use of the thin outlines of tertiary shapes. Even here, in some of the most sensitive paintings, the space between this line and the primary or secondary form it follows is not constant in width, thus conforming to the idea of nonparallelism or nonconcentricity.

Transition

Easy transition from form to form throughout the design is characteristic of the art. Primarily, this is accomplished by the use of

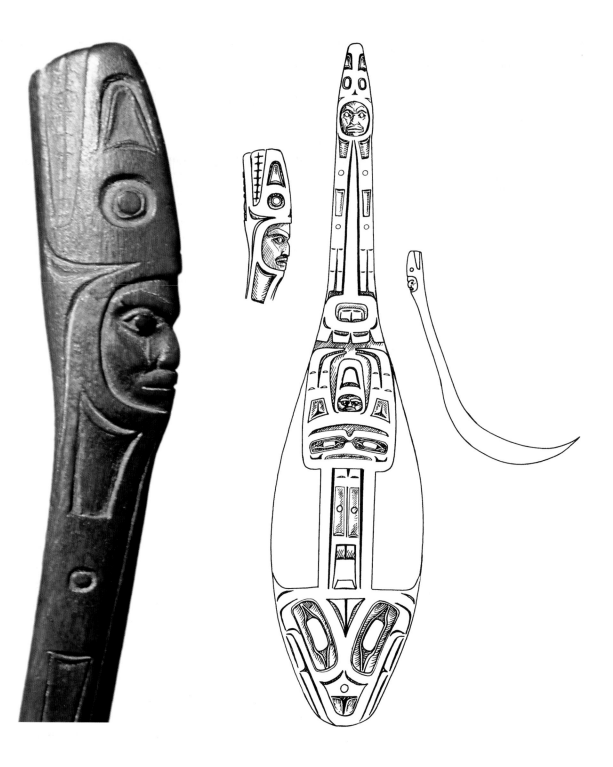

70 Mountain sheep horn spoon.
Private collection.

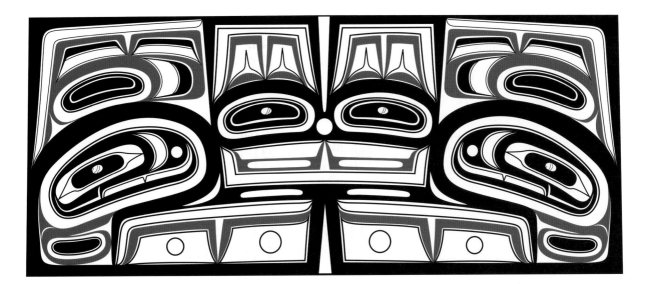

71 Painted box front, Bella Bella. The Field Museum 79389.

the transitional devices described. Another method of facilitating transition and flow of movement is the staggering of tangent corners. That is to say, ovoids or other units rarely join corner to corner, but join near the corners at their sides. The formlines of units joined at their corners form an intersection which interferes with the easy fluidity of the composition and seems usually to have been avoided.

Double Meaning

The similarity of body-part designs makes the use of these units in double symbolism possible and relatively common. The Bella Coola seemed especially to enjoy this byplay, particularly in masks and poles. Fins, ears, and feet often take the form of birds' heads. The fact that eye and joint designs are indistinguishable makes this possible. The claws of a foot, or the curve of a flipper, becomes the beak of the bird whose eye is suggested by the joint design. The joints of the two shoulders become the eyes of a face which fills the body area, provided with ears, mouth, and nose. The well-known salmon-on-trout's-head and double-eye designs are merely elaborations of ovoids into facelike patterns. The famous "Rain Wall" at Klukwan (Fig. 67 and Emmons, 1916:Pl. 2) is literally covered with over fifty such extraneous faces, many of them fitted out with little bodies, arms, and legs. The tails of whales are often elaborated into faces because of the similarity of the fluke designs to ears. Since this use of double meaning certainly exists, it is tempting to read it into

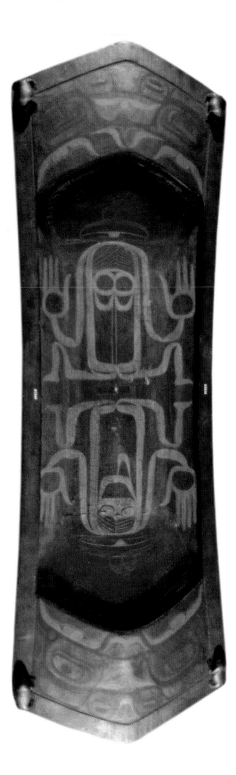

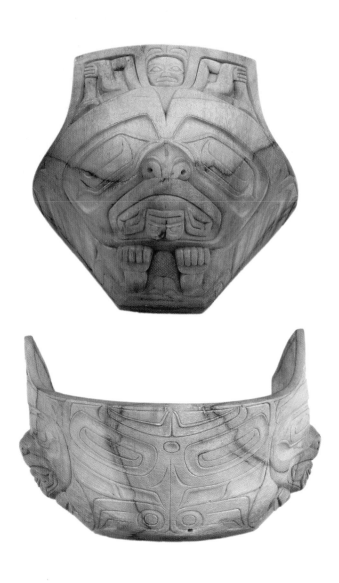

72 Painted food tray. The Field Museum
14424.

73 Carved bowl of mountain sheep horn.
Burke Museum catalogue number 1-3003.

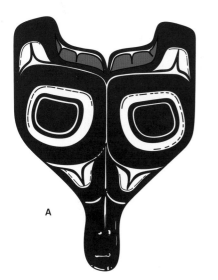
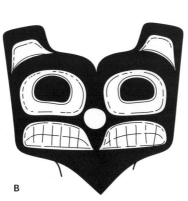
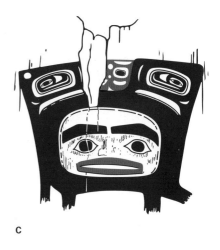

74 Whale tails. (A) From a Tlingit mask. Burke Museum catalogue number 1-11395. (B) From a Bella Bella clapper. Royal British Columbia Museum 122. (C) From a Tlingit house post. Portland Art Museum 48.3.529.

examples where it might be only imagined. The intent of the artist may be judged by the position of joints relative to flukes. If the concave or lower side of the joint adjoins the base of the fluke, as in Figure 74A, it could hardly be interpreted as an eye, since it would be upside down in relation to the ear (fluke). Still, the arrangement suggests a face, and it is easy to imagine the process by which the Indian artist modified these forms toward progressively more realistic representations (Fig. 74B). The examples shown do not imply a chronological sequence (Figure 74C may in fact be the earliest), but they illustrate the possible evolution of the extraneous face in body, joint, and filler designs.

Even such astute observers as Emmons may have been misled by what seemed to have been intended as a double meaning. Emmons wrote of a silver bracelet (Fig. 75), "A peculiar feature of the legs and feet—really an artist's licence—is the head of an Eagle while the miniature feet of the Beaver appear underneath the upper bill of the eagle . . ." (collection note, Denver Art Museum). It seems very doubtful to me that the artist intended anything other than a typical handling of the beaver's legs and feet.

Nevertheless, a great deal of double meaning was introduced into such formalized designs, suggesting a very versatile imagination and perhaps a keen sense of humor on the part of the artists.

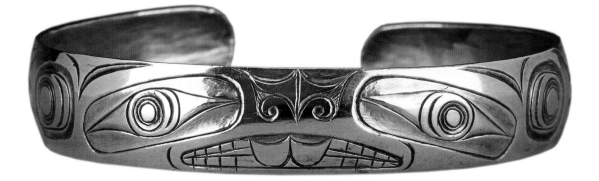

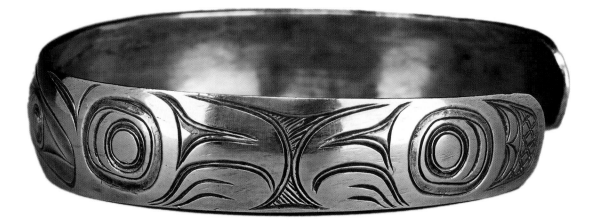

75 Silver bracelet with a beaver design,
Haida. Attributed to Charles Edensaw,
bracelet, c.1900, Denver Art Museum
Collection: Purchase from G. T. Emmons,
1941.137. Photograph © Denver Art
Museum.

Space Fillers

In an art so strongly characterized by even distribution of weight and movement, the importance of the space-filling element becomes obvious. Essential body parts could be elaborated and empty areas filled with units that elsewhere in the design had specific and entirely different symbolism. The use of these at times meaningful design units for purely decorative purposes is an important principle of this art.

Conclusions

IT IS APPARENT THAT THERE WAS, ON THE NORTHWEST COAST, a highly developed system for the organization of form and space in two-dimensional design as an adjunct to the well-known symbolism. Design ranging from nearly realistic representation to abstraction resulted from the application of the principles of this system. Chief among these principles was the concept of a continuous primary formline pattern delineating the main shapes and elaborated with secondary complexes and isolated tertiary elements. Also important to it was a formalized color usage that prescribed the placement of the three principal colors: black, red, and blue-green. There was a set series of design units which could be arranged and varied in proportion to fit the requirements of space and representation. Important among these were the formline, the formline ovoid, and the U form. To define forms and to maintain the fluidity of design, a group of transitional devices was used. Monotony was minimized by nonconcentricity and avoidance of parallels, as well as by firm semiangularity of curves. A limit to the degree of elaboration was imposed which was independent of the scale of the design.

The total effect of the system was to produce a strong, yet sensitive, division of the given shape by means of an interlocking formline pattern of shapes related in form, color, and scale.

Although it is beyond the scope of this study to deal with the possible origins of development of Northwest Coast two-dimensional art, an interesting possibility of a close kinesthetic relationship of this art to dance movement is worth mentioning. Boas (1927:335) has suggested that there are relationships of this kind:

> Dance contains elements of both the spatial and time arts.
> Therefore, the principles of the former may be clearly observed
> in dance forms. Rhythmic movements and rhythmic spatial
> order, symmetry of position and movement, and emphasis and
> balance of form are essential in esthetic dance form.

I, myself, have derived a certain physical satisfaction from the muscle activity involved in producing the characteristic line movement of this art, and there can be little doubt that this was true also for the Indian artist. To say that there may be a kinesthetic relationship between this movement and dance movement is not to say that there is any visual or spatial similarity, although there may be, but to a lesser degree. Because of the purely sensory nature of the suggested relationship, it is difficult, if not impossible, for one who has not personally participated in both activities to be aware of it.

Some of the most skillful artists of the southern Kwakiutl are also among the best dancers and song composers, a situation that probably was also true of the northern tribes during their heyday. The interrelationship of the arts has been recognized in other cultures. An East Indian treatise of the sixth century A.D. describes a conversation in which a sage advises a king that he must first learn the theory of dancing before he can learn the whole meaning of art, since the laws of dancing imply the principles that govern painting (Kramrisch, 1954:9).

The constant flow of movement, broken at rhythmic intervals by rather sudden, but not necessarily jerky, changes of motion-direction, characterizes both the dance and art of the Northwest Coast.

Whatever the origins of the art may have been, it is certain that no system could ever, of itself, produce the masterworks of Northwest Coast art which are the inspiration and the object of this study. As in all art it remained for the imagination and sensitivity of some of the most imaginative and sensitive of men to give life to a list of rules and principles and produce the wonderful compositions that came from the northern coast. It is precisely because each piece was the creation of the mind of a man that it can be analyzed only superficially in terms of elements and principles, while that quality which raises the best of Northwest Coast design to the status of art remains unmeasured.

Appendix

ALTHOUGH 400 KEYSORT CARDS WERE PREPARED AS A BASIS for this study, 392 specimens are actually represented, since two cards were made for such pieces as the large chests with the ends painted only and the sides painted and carved. Provision was made for the recording of any information that seemed pertinent, on the basis of many years of observation and deep personal interest in the art. Even so, a number of possible design characteristics were left out in the preparation of the check list, and those that were recognized as the study progressed were entered on the cards as marginal notes.

Figure 76 shows a typical card, recorded and punched for the carved and painted sides of the chest shown in Figure 77. The symbols on the card refer to the surface form of the given design element in cross section.

The symbols are marked opposite the appropriate element in the column which corresponds to the color with which that element is painted. If an element occurs in more than one color or surface form, symbols indicating those characteristics are included. Elements occurring on the flat surface of the decorated area are indicated with a straight horizontal line —. This line is sometimes preceded by a hatching or dashing symbol if the element is so decorated. Elements that are recessed with a rounded concave surface are indicated by a curved line ⌣ and those whose recessed surface is beveled are marked with a check √. Elements occurring in anything other than black, red, blue-green, or the natural color of the material used are listed in the "Other" column. An example in Figure 77 is the use of abalone shell for some of the inner ovoids (ab in the "Other" column on the card, Fig. 76).

Line T, "Contin," records the characteristic of continuity or the lack of it in the three classes of design elements: primary, secondary, and tertiary. The illustrated card was checked to indicate that the specimen exhibited primary and secondary continuity and isolation of tertiary elements. This is a typical case. Of the specimens studied, 399/400 have primary continuity, 399/400 have secondary continuity, and 387/400 have complete isolation of tertiary elements.

Line U, "Odds," records the occurrence of three characteristics not covered in the lines above. The first, "Eye U," refers to the design described on page 41 and shown in Figure 31A. The next space refers to the three-dimensional intrusion described on page 18 and shown, for example, in Figures 13 and 14. The last space, "Pri-Sec

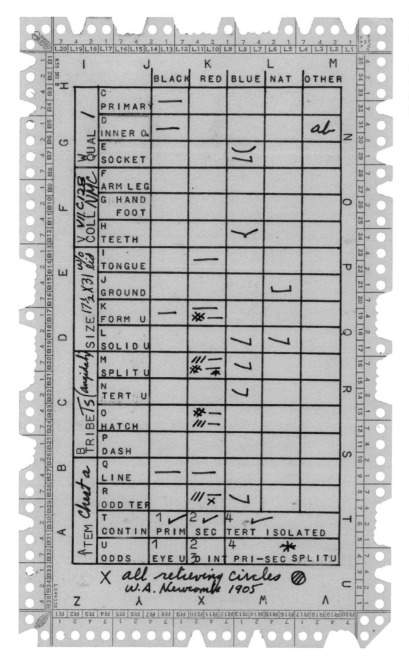

76 Sample Keysort card recorded from the chest illustrated in Fig. 77.

77 Four sides of a carved and painted chest, Tsimshian. Canadian Museum of History, catalogue number VII C 128, image numbers S94-6792, S94-6793.

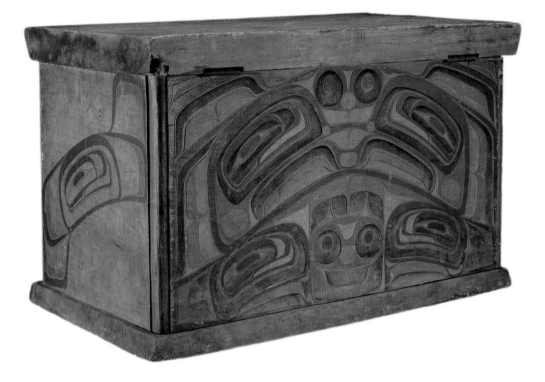

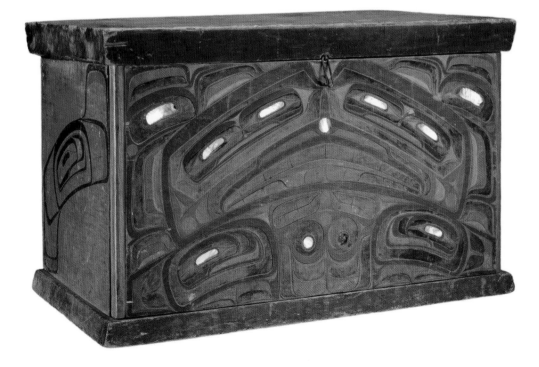

Split U," records the occurrence of the relatively uncommon (50/400) primary-secondary split U. In the card shown in Figure 76 the asterisk refers back to line M, "Split U," where the primary-secondary split U's are shown to have been flat and hatched in red.

Any other information recorded from the specimen or its documentation, but not shown elsewhere on the card, was written in the space below line U. The card illustrated records the facts that relieving circles were hatched (in red, according to the symbols in line R, "Odd Tert") and that W. A. Newcombe was the collector in 1905. Other information on the cards gives the specimen; its tribal and village origin, if known; size; present location; catalogue number; and quality. In an effort to eliminate subjective judgment from the recording of characteristics, the quality of a specimen was rated on the basis of craftsmanship only. The most perfectly finished examples with sharp, clean lines, smooth curves, symmetrical ovoids, and the like were rated 1. Those specimens showing the poorest workmanship were rated 4. Others fell between these extremes. Admittedly this system is imperfect, but it allows an opportunity to consider any relationship there might be between skilled craftsmanship, which perhaps implies the training and experience of an accepted professional, and adherence to the principles described herein.

Much of the information recorded is shown in the three tables. Numerals indicate the incidence of each design characteristic. For example in Table 1, section C (Primary): of 160 specimens, 133 had exclusively black primary design, 22 had only red primary, and 5 had both black and red; this is shown by the dots in the black and red columns. Occurrence of hatching is indicated by ⦀, and ▦, and dashing by ⹀. Notes in parentheses explain other characteristics.

It is possible that some important bits of information have been missed in the recording, and no doubt considerably more could be derived from the cards, especially in regard to the incidence of one characteristic in relation to others. The information recorded was not always complete for each specimen, since in some cases time limitations prevented reference to museum records of collection data. Also, some of the specimens included could not be removed from their display cases, and consequently part of the decorated area was not seen. There are only a few such objects included in this study, however, and it is unlikely that the unseen designs would have appreciably affected the tabulation. Moreover, many of the

78 Cross section of a carving. Some of the symbols used on the Keysort cards and in Tables 1–3 are shown below the surface characteristics they represent.

pieces examined were photographed, which permitted reexamination, comparison, and checking on conclusions.

The specimens recorded on cards are a random sampling of many more pieces seen during years of interest in Northwest Coast Indian art. It has been found that the vast majority of two-dimensional decorated objects in collections of Northwest Coast material do conform to the tenants of organization described here.

TABLE 1 Characteristics of Specimens That Were Painted Only

160 Specimens PAINTED ONLY	BLACK	RED	BLUE	NATURAL	OTHER
C. Primary 160	133 •————	22 ——•5			
D. Iris Ovoid 160	156 •————	•1 ——•————	•1 ——•————	•1 ——•1	
E. Sockets 160	4 (black ground) •————		9	132 •1 (a copper) •6	2 (white ground) •9 ≡≡ ⁄⁄ ▨ (in ext. faces) 1≡≡(Kwakiutl)
F. Arm Leg 68	30 •————	35 ——•3			
G. Hand Foot 73	39 •————	28 ——•6 (1 with black claws, red ovoid)			
H. Teeth 85	12 •————	17 •1 ——•————	2	48 (40 blackout 8 (redout) •5 (redout)	
I. Tongue 82	14 •———— ⁄⁄2	60 ——•1 ⁄⁄2		3	
J. Ground 160	4 •———— ——•————			155 ——•1 ——•3	3 (white)
K. Formline U 160	13 •————	6 (3 appliqué) ——•141			
L. Solid U 155	5 •———— ——•———— ——•————	15 ——•2 ——•3	5 •————	101 ——•1 ——•7 ——•4 ——•6	•3▨black •3▨red
M. Split U 139	•————	9 ——•————	8 •————	99 ——•1 ——•1 ——•2	1 (white ground) •▨——•1 (white ground) ——•17▨
N. Tertiary U 26	1 (a copper)		5	18	2 (white ground)
O. Hatching 86	34 •————	26 ——•26			
P. Dashing 40	23 •————	13 ——•3	1 (Kwakiutl)		
Q. Line 159	49 •———— ——•————	3 (1 appliqué) ——•106 •————	(Kwakiutl)		1 (no line, appliqué)
R. Odd Tert. 41		1 (relief-ovoid) •————	5 ——•———— ——•1	24 ——•———— •————	5⁄⁄ •2⁄⁄ •2 2 (white)⁄⁄
T. Continuity 160	Primary 160	Secondary 160	Tert. Isolated 160		
U. Odds	Eye U 9	3-D Intrusion 3	Pri-Sec Split U 27		
	BLACK	RED			
X. ▨ Formline U 69	27 •————	27 ——•15			
Y. ▨ Solid U 28	16 •————	9 ——•3			
Z. ▨ Split U	11 •————	6 ——•2			

TABLE 2 Characteristics of Specimens That Were Carved Only

131 Specimens CARVED ONLY	—	⌐‾	‿	XXXX	OTHER
C. Primary 131	128		•1 ‾‿ •1	•1	
D. Inner Ovoid 131	123		•1 ‾	1	1 (abalone) •5 (abalone)
E. Sockets 131		21	78 •32		
F. Arm Leg 57	53			1	1 (3-D) •2 (3-D)
G. Hand Foot 68	64			1	2 (3-D) •1 (3-D)
H. Teeth 81	35	26 (3 v, 2⌄⌄) •5	10 •1 ‾	1	2 (abalone) •1 (abalone)
I. Tongue 34	20	8	3 ‾	1	1 (abalone) 1 ∧
J. Ground 124	2	48 ✓ ⌐ v •2		50 •5 •7	17 (no ground except V)
K. Formline U 131	128			2 •1	
L. Solid U	24	10 •11	18 •15 •5 •2	10 — 1✓ 1⌣ •4 •4 •2 •3 •3 •1 •1	3 (abalone)
M. Split U 72	2	12 ✓ 1⌣	35 •1 •4	11 1⌣ •5	
N. Tertiary U 54		18	32 •1	2 •1	
O. Hatching 73	71 •1		•1		
P. Dashing 21	21				
Q. Line 131	131				
R. Odd Tert. 50		3 •4	41	•2 (tert. ovoid)	
T. Continuity 131	Primary 130	Secondary 130	Tert. Isolated 118		
U. Odds 40	Eye U 3	3-D Intrusion 27	Pri-Sec Split U 7 •2 •1		

X. ⊠ Formline U	8	—
Y. ⊠ Solid U	29	—
Z. ⊠ Split U	14	—
Incised Ground	62	⊠//

TABLE 3 Characteristics of Specimens That Were Carved and Painted

109 Specimens CARVED-PAINTED	BLACK	RED	BLUE	NATURAL	OTHER
C. Primary 109	96 —	12 — ● 1 —			
D. Inner Ovoid 109	90 —	4 — ● 3 —		● 1 — ● 1 —	5 — (abalone) ● 5 — (abalone & copper)
E. Sockets 109			10 ⌣ 32 ⌣ 16 ⌣ 1 ⌣ (½ painted only) ● 2 ● 2 ⌣ ● 1 ⌣ ⌣ ● 1 ⌣	6 ⌣) No 25 ⌣ } Blue on 13 ⌣) Specimen	
F. Arm Leg 45	19 — 1 ⌒ ●	19 — 2 ⌒ ● 2 — ●		● 1 ⌒ ● 1 ⌒ (copper)	
G. Hand Foot 50	15 — 1 ⌒ ●	25 — 3 ⌒ ● 3 —		1 — 2 ⌒	
H. Teeth 63	7 — ●	9 — 1 ⌣	10 ⌣ 1 ⌣	3 — 19 ⌣ 3 ⌣ 2 ⌣ 1 ⌒ ● 1 ⌣ ● 1 ⌣ ⌣ ● 1 (abalone)	2 (abalone) 2 (opercula)
I. Tongue 57	1 — 1 /// —	34 — 18 ⌒	1 — 2 ⌣ (1 was repainted) 1 ⌒	1 ⌣ 2 ⌒	
J. Ground 109		1 ⌣	1 ⌣ 2 ⌣ 1 ⌒	22 ⌣ 60 ⌣ 6 ⌣ 2 ※ v 13 v ● 1 ⌣	
K. Formline U 109	15 — ●	5 — ● 85 — ● ● 3 ※ —		● 1 — (a dish painted on ends only)	

TABLE 3 (continued)

109 Specimens
CARVED-PAINTED

	BLACK	RED	BLUE	NATURAL	OTHER
L. Solid U 97 (includes 17 ordinary combinations not shown in this table)	2—	11— 1⊗∨	10∨ 6∪ 4∪ •1∪ •— —• •1∨ •∪ — •— —•3∪ •— —•6∪ •— —•2∨ •— —•3∪ •— — —•1⊔	16∨ 9∪ •3∪ •2∨ •3∪	•1 (abalone)
M. Split U 61	•/// — —•1∪	4∪	20∪ 7∨ 2∪ •1∨ •∪ —•1∪ •— —•1∪	12∪ 8∨ 1—inc⊗ 1∪inc⊗ 1∪ 1∨inc⊗	
N. Tertiary U 27			5∪ 4∨ 1—	13∪ 2∨ 1— 1∪	
O. Hatching 21	1— •— — — —	1— •8—	•— — — — — —	10—inc •1—inc	
P. Dashing 3		1—	1(?)—	1(?)—	
Q. Line 109	67— •— — — —	3— •39—			
R. Odd Tert. 54		1∨ •/// — —•1∨	17∪ 3 •1∨	27∪ (only 1 of these has any blue) 2⊔ 1∨ 1∪ •— — —•1∪	

	Primary	Secondary	Tert. Isolated		
T. Continuity 109	109	109	107		

	Eye U	3-D Intrusion	Pri-Sec Split U		
U. Odds 36	4 •— — — — —•2 •— — — —•2	17 — —•2 •— —•2	9		

	BLACK	RED	INCISED
X.⊗ Formline U 14	6—	1— •5—	1— •— —•1
Y.⊗ Solid U 8	1—	6—	1—
Z.⊗ Split U 6	2—	1—	3—
⊗ Incised Ground 7 (all dishes)	—		

Bibliography

Adam, L.

1929   *Nordwest-Amerikanische Indianerkunst.* Orbis Pictus, Vol. XVII. Berlin: E. Wasmuth.

1936   "North-West American Indian Art and Its Early Chinese Parallels," *Man,* Vol. XXXVI, No. 3.

Barbeau, Marius

1939   "Indian Silversmiths on the Pacific Coast," *Proceedings and Transactions of the Royal Society of Canada,* Ser. 3, Vol. XXXIII, No. 2, pp. 23–28.

1950   *Totem Poles.* Anthropological Series No. 30, Bulletin 119, Vols. I and II. National Museum of Canada, Ottawa.

1953   *Haida Myths Illustrated in Argillite Carvings.* Anthropological Series No. 32, Bulletin 127. National Museum of Canada, Ottawa.

1957   *Haida Carvers.* Anthropological Series No. 38, Bulletin 139. National Museum of Canada, Ottawa.

Boas, Franz

1897   *The Decorative Art of the Indians of the North Pacific Coast.* Bulletin of the American Museum of Natural History, Vol. IX, pp. 123–76.

1900   *Facial Paintings of the Indians of Northern British Columbia.* Memoirs of the American Museum of Natural History, Vol. II, pp. 13–24.

1909   *The Kwakiutl of Vancouver Island.* Memoirs of the American Museum of Natural History, Vol. VIII, pp. 307–515.

1927   *Primitive Art.* Oslo: Aschehoug.

British Columbia Indian Arts and Welfare Society

1948   *Native Designs of British Columbia.* Victoria.

Covarrubias, Miguel

1954   *The Eagle, the Jaguar, and the Serpent.* New York: Alfred A. Knopf.

Davis, Robert T.

1949   *Native Arts of the Pacific Northwest.* Stanford, Calif.: Stanford University Press.

Dawson, G. M.

1880   *Report on the Queen Charlotte Islands.* Geological Survey of Canada, Report of Progress for 1878–79, pp. 1B-239B.

Dixon, George

1789   *A Voyage Round the World.* London: G. Goulding.

Dockstader, Frederick J.

1961   *Indian Art in America.* Greenwich, Conn.: New York Graphic Society.

Duff, Wilson

1956   "Prehistoric Stone Sculpture of the Fraser River and the Gulf of Georgia," *Anthropology in British Columbia,* No. 5. Victoria.

1964   "Contributions of Marius Barbeau to West Coast Ethnology," *Anthropologica,* N.S., Vol. VI, No. 1.

Emmons, George T.

1907   *The Chilkat Blanket*. Memoirs of the American Museum of Natural History, Vol. Ill, pp. 329–400.

1916   *The Whale House of the Chilkat*. Anthropological Papers of the American Museum of Natural History, Vol. XIX, pp. 1–33.

1930   "The Art of the Northwest Coast Indians," *Natural History*, Vol. XXX, pp. 282–92.

Feder, Norman, and Edward Malin

1962   *Indian Art of the Northwest Coast*. Denver Art Museum Quarterly, Winter, 1962.

Fraser, Douglas

1962   *Primitive Art*. Garden City, N.Y.: Doubleday and Co.

Garfield, Viola

1955a   "Making a Bird or Chiefs' Rattle," *Davidson Journal of Anthropology*, Vol. I, No. 2, pp. 155–64.

1955b   "Making a Box Design," *Davidson Journal of Anthropology*, Vol. I, No. 2, pp. 165–68.

Gunther, Erna

1951   *Indians of the Northwest Coast*. Colorado Springs and Seattle.

1962   *Northwest Coast Indian Art*. Seattle.

Haeberlin, Hermann K.

1918   "Principles of Esthetic Form in the Art of the North Pacific Coast," *American Anthropologist*, N.S., Vol. XX, pp. 258–64.

Heizer, Robert

1940   "The Introduction of Monterey Shells to the Indians of the Northwest Coast," *Pacific Northwest Quarterly*, October, 1940.

Inverarity, Robert Bruce

1946   *Northwest Coast Indian Art*. Washington State Museum, University of Washington, Museum Series, No. 1.

1950   *Art of the Northwest Coast Indians*. Berkeley: University of California Press.

Keithahn, Edward L.

1962   "Heraldic Screens of the Tlingit," *Alaska Sportsman*, Vol. XXVIII, No. 2.

1963   *Monuments in Cedar*. Seattle: Superior Press.

Kramrisch, Stella

1954   *The Art of India: Traditions of Indian Sculpture, Painting and Architecture*. London.

Krickeberg, Walter

1925   "Malereien auf ledernen Zeremonialkleidern der Nordwestamerikaner," *IPEK*, pp. 140–50.

Leechman, Douglas
1932   "Aboriginal Paints and Dyes in Canada," *Proceedings and Transactions of the Royal Society of Canada*, Ser. 3, Vol. XXVI, No. 2, pp. 37–42.
1942   "Abalone Shells from Monterey," *American Anthropologist*, N.S., Vol. XLIV, pp. 159–62.

Levi-Strauss, Claude
1943   "The Art of the Northwest Coast at the American Museum of Natural History," *Gazette des Beaux-Arts*, Vol. XXIV, pp. 175–82.

MacCallum, Spencer
1955   "American Indian Art of the North Pacific Coast." Unpublished thesis for the degree of Bachelor of Arts, Department of Art and Archeology, Princeton University.

Marchand, Etienne
1801   *A Voyage Round the World*. London: T. N. Longman and O. Rees.

Niblack, Albert P.
1888   *The Coast Indians of Southern Alaska and Northern British Columbia*. Report of the United States National Museum, pp. 225–386.

Paalen, Wolfgang
1943   "Totem Art," *DYN*, Nos. 4–5. Mexico, D.F.

Royal Ontario Museum
1959   *Masks, the Many Faces of Man*. Toronto.

Scott, Robert G.
1951   *Design Fundamentals*. New York: McGraw-Hill Co.

Shotridge, Louis
1919   "War Helmets and Clan Hats of the Tlingit Indians," *Museum Journal*, University of Pennsylvania, Vol. X, pp. 43–48.
1929   "The Kagwanton Shark Helmet," *Museum Journal*, University of Pennsylvania, Vol. XX.

Sloan, John, and Oliver LaFarge
1931   *Introduction to American Indian Art*. The Exposition of American Tribal Arts, Inc., New York.

Swan, James G.
1874   "The Haidah Indians of Queen Charlotte's Islands," *Smithsonian Contributions to Knowledge*, Vol. XVI, No. 4, pp. 1–15.

Swanton, John R.
1908   *Social Condition, Beliefs and Linguistic Relationship of the Tlingit Indians*. 26th Annual Report of the Bureau of American Ethnology.
1909   *Contributions to the Ethnology of the Haida*. Memoirs of the American Museum of Natural History, Vol. VIII.

Utzinger, Rudolf
    1922   *Masken*. Orbis Pictus, Vol. XIII. Berlin: E. Wasmuth.

Von Sydow, Eckart
    1932   *Die Kunst der Naturvölker und der Vorzeit*. Berlin: Propyläen-Verlag.

Waterman, T. T.
    1923   "Some Conundrums in Northwest Coast Art," *American Anthropologist*, N.S., Vol. XXV, pp. 435–51.

Willett, Frank
    1961   "A Set of Gambling Pegs from the Northwest Coast of America," *Man*, Vol. LXI, Articles 1–25, pp. 8–10 with Plate D.

Wingert, Paul
    1951   "Tsimshian Sculpture," *The Tsimshian: Their Arts and Music*. Vol. XVIII, Publications of the American Ethnological Society. Seattle: University of Washington Press.

Index

A

abalone shell, 19, 30

Adam, Leonhard, 8

Alaska: Klukwan, xxv, 6, 22; Klukwan Clan Houses, 6; Klukwan Whale House interior, 83*fig*.63; Russian contact in, 3

Alaska Indian Arts, Haines, xix

antler, as material, 14

appliqué: negative shapes in, 79; as technique, 19, 30; woolen shirt, Haida, 81*fig*.64

argillite (black slate): argillite chest, Haida, xxvi; argillite platter, Haida, 22*fig*.16; as material, 14

arms designs, color of, 30

artists: as dancers and composers, 93; individual style of, 23; Kwakiutl, xxvii, 69, 93. *See also* Edensaw, Charles; Martin, Mungo; Price, Tom; principles of form and organization

asymmetric design, 84

B

background. *See* ground

balance, 71

beads in appliqué, 19

beaver motives: Edensaw silver bracelet, 89, 90*fig*.75; woven spruce hat, Haida, 12*fig*.7

Bella Bella (Heiltsuk): cobalt dashing by, 64–65; fragment of painted coffin, xxvii*fig*.3; intertribal variations and, 20–21; mask, biaxial symmetry in, 85; whale tale from clapper, 89*fig*.74B

Bella Coola (Nuxalk): cobalt dashing by, 65; color use, 26; double meaning and, 87–89; face mask, 23, 24*fig*.17B; mask decoration style, 23; northern style, limit of, 8; painted skin blanket, 17; totem pole decoration style, 25

biaxial symmetry, 85

black: as primary color, 28*fig*.21A, 29–30, 29*fig*.D–E; as principal color, 26

black slate. *See* argillite

blankets: color in, 30; painted skin blanket, Bella Coola, 17. *See also* Chilkat blanket

blue-green: as ground color, 57; as principal color, 26; as tertiary color, 29*fig*.21C–E, 32–33

Boas, Franz, 8, 9, 65, 69, 75, 84

bone, as material, 14

bowls: biaxial symmetry and, 85; carved bowl of mountain sheep horn, 88*fig*.73; carved wooden bowl, Haida, 3, 4*fig*.4A–C; carved wooden grease dish, Haida, 47*fig*.37; frog bowl, Haida, 17*fig*.13; Northern Northwest Coast bentwood bowl, xx*fig*.

boxes: Bill Reid consulting Bill Holm on, xx; carved and painted box, Haida, 20; design process, 67–69, 70*fig*.56; designs from sides of, 79*fig*.62; four sides of square box, Massett Haida, 77*fig*.60; full-face square boxes, design organization of, 75–76, 77*fig*.60, 78*fig*.61, 79*fig*.62; painted box front, Kwakiutl, 87*fig*.71; relation of total organization to unit design, 74*fig*.59

bracelets, silver: catalogued as Tsimshian, 21–22; Edensaw bracelets, Haida, 80, 82*fig*.65–66, 90*fig*.75; Emmons' description of, 89; engraved silver bracelet, Haida, 73*fig*.58; engraved silver bracelet with hatching, Tlingit, 63*fig*.52C; Haida, 15*fig*.10

brushes for painting, 28

buttons in appliqué, 19

79*fig.*62; movement, 83–84; nonconcentricity, 85; positive-negative space, 76, 79–83; semiangularity of curves, 84; simplicity, relative, 73–75; space fillers, 91; standardized design organization in other decorated objects, 76, 80*fig.*63; symmetry, 84–85; total use of given space, 67; transition, 85–87; unit form, relation to, 74*fig.*59, 75

principles of representation, 8–9, 20–21

provenience, 21–22

Q

quillwork as technique, 19

R

Rain Wall at Klukwan, xxv, 80–81, 87

rattles, 18*fig.*14, 80*fig.*63

raven rattles, 80*fig.*63

Raven Screens, Huna Tlingit, xxiv*fig.*1, xxv, 6

realism, degrees of, 9–12, 71

red: on convex surfaces, 32; dashing in, 64; in inner ovoid, 30; as principal color, 26; as secondary color, 28*fig.*21B, 29*fig.*D–E, 30–32

Reid, Bill, xx, xxvii

relief: of claw designs, 49; of fluidity, 83; of inner ovoids, 58, 61, 61*fig.*50, 62*fig.*51; of junctures, 57, 58*fig.*47B; of U forms, 41

relief carving: after painting, 33; color and, 30, 32, 33; as decorative treatment on wood, 14; tribal style variations, 23, 25. *See also* totem poles

representation, principles of, 8–9, 20–21

resultant forms, 57

rhythmic emphasis, 84

right-angle junctures, 58, 60*fig.*49

Roblet, Surgeon, 6–7

Russian contact in Alaska, 3

S

Saanich: northern chest collected from, 22

sailing ships, in trade period, 19

Salish, 20

salmon eggs as paint medium, 28

salmon-trout's-head ovoids: color of, 40; construction of, 49*fig.*39; examples of, 32*fig.*23, 34*fig.*24; on Haida totem pole detail, 35*fig.*25; joints and, 37; name of, xxi; organization, compared to faces, 45; on square boxes, 75

Samuel, Cheryl, xvii

schematization of form, weaving and, 20

sea wolf painted in Boas' *Primitive Art*, 65

secondary color, 28*fig.*21B, 29*fig.*D–E, 30–32, 49

secondary complexes, 30, 71, 76

secondary continuants, 30

secondary elements: continuity and, 81; L forms, 47;

negative shapes and, 80; simplicity and, 73; texture in, 61; U forms, 40–41, 40*fig.*30, 47, 47*fig.*37

secondary formlines, 30–32, 71

semiangular curves, 35, 81, 84

Sendey, John, 23

S forms, 43, 43*fig.*33, 47*fig.*37

shaman paraphernalia, paintings on, 11

Shotridge, Louis, 26

silver, Haida work in, 80

silver bracelets. *See* bracelets, silver

simplicity, 73–75, 76, 81

single-eye form: example of, 46*fig.*36; as "one-step structure," xxi

skate markings, 37

sketching, preliminary, 67–69

skins: dance leggings, Haida, 17–18; painted skin kilt, 36*fig.*26; painted skin blanket, 17; painting on, 14, 17

slate. *See* argillite

sockets. *See* eye sockets

solid U's: as secondary element, 40–41; as tertiary element, 32

space, organization of. *See* principles of form and organization

space fillers, 91

split U's, 32, 41–42, 41*fig.*31, 61

spoons: carved soapberry spoon with hatching, Tlingit, 63*fig.*52B; flat design on spoon bowls, 18; mountain sheep horn spoon, 86*fig.*70; painted wooden spoon, Stikine Tlingit, 27*fig.*19; "unwrapped" spoon handle designs, 16*fig.*11A–C

spruce hat, woven, Tlingit, 13*fig.*8

spruce hats, woven, Haida, 12*fig.*6–7, 22–23

spruce root mat painting, Haida, 27*fig.*19

square boxes. *See* boxes

square junctures, 57

Stephens, Godfrey (Goof), xviii–xix

stone, as material, 14

straight junctures, 57

stylized face, 43, 44*fig.*35A

subsecondary elements, 30, 40, 71–73

surface, adaptation of form to, 67

Swan, James G., 35

Swanton, John R., 9

swelling junctures, 58

symbolism, 8–9, 75

symmetry, 37, 84–85

T

tapering junctures, 45

techniques: painting, 14; relief carving, 14; weaving and appliqué, 19, 20

templates: cardboard, 67; folded, 37; symmetry and, 85; tracings of ovoid templates, 31*fig.*22; use of, 35, 45, 76

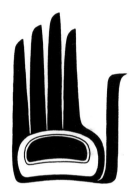